FINDING
CHRIST
IN THE
STRAW

A Forty-Day Devotion on the Epistle of James

FINDING
CHRIST
IN THE
STRAW

A Forty-Day Devotion on the Epistle of James

ROBERT M. HILLER

1517 Publishing

Finding Christ in the Straw: A Forty-Day Devotion on the Epistle of James

© 2020 Robert M. Hiller

Published by:
1517 Publishing
PO Box 54032
Irvine, CA 92619-4032

Publisher's Cataloging-In-Publication Data
(Prepared by The Donohue Group, Inc.)

Names: Hiller, Robert M., author.
Title: Finding Christ in the straw : a forty-day devotion on the
        Epistle of James / by Robert M. Hiller.
Description: Irvine, CA : 1517 Publishing, [2019] | Includes bibliographical references.
Identifiers: ISBN 9781948969154 (softcover) | ISBN 9781948969161 (ebook)
Subjects: LCSH: Bible. James—Devotional use. | Jesus Christ—Prayers and devotions.
        | Devotional exercises. | LCGFT: Devotional literature.
Classification: LCC BS2785.4 .H55 2019 (print) | LCC BS2785.4 (ebook) | DDC 242/.5—dc23

Printed in the United States of America

Cover art by Brenton Clarke Little

Dedicated to
Stephanie, Sophie, Mark, and Tim.

"Every good gift and every perfect gift is from above, coming down from the Father of lights with whom there is no variation or shadow due to change" (Jas. 1:17).

You are gifts God has given me. I praise Him for you.

And
the saints at Faith Lutheran Church in Moorpark, California, and Community Lutheran Church in Escondido/San Marcos, California. Thank you for showing me God's grace and teaching me to preach.

CONTENTS

INTRODUCTION

A number of years ago, a friend of mine suggested we do a sermon series where we gave a daily challenge to our congregation. At first, I was worried such a practice might border on legalism. But then the idea began to grow on me. Yet where in the world would we draw such inspiration for such an endeavor? Then it struck me—the Epistle of James! After all, James is all about good works as the fruit of faith, right? So, if we are going to challenge our congregations to work, we might as well use the book that has the most law. Right?

I am a Lutheran pastor. We Lutherans have a bit of a funny relationship to old James. Martin Luther, you may recall, once referred to this New Testament letter—written by the brother of our Lord—as "an epistle of straw."[1] Luther felt that this letter lacked the focus on the person and work of Jesus Christ to warrant much of his energy. Straw has its benefits but is not all that useful in the long run. Traditionally, the Lutheran "canon within the canon" focuses on the works of St. Paul, especially Romans and Galatians, where Paul destroys any hope of life or salvation in our own works. Paul is clear: "For we hold that one is justified (declared righteous before God) by faith apart from works of the law" (Rom. 3:28).

---

1. "Therefore, St. James' epistle is really an epistle of straw, compared to these others, for it has nothing of the nature of the gospel about it." Martin Luther, "Prefaces to the New Testament," in *Martin Luther's Basic Theological Writings*, ed. Timothy Lull (Minneapolis: Fortress, 1989), 117.

In a time when the church was exalting the glorious works of man and demanding faith in such works for salvation, Luther found it necessary to recover these particular words of the Holy Spirit. Justification by grace alone, through faith alone, and on account of Christ alone was the battle cry!

But then along comes the brother of Jesus, James himself, saying, "You see that a person is justified by works and not by faith alone" (Jas. 2:24). Further study of the text will show that Paul and James both hold to salvation apart from works for Christ's sake alone. But the way James speaks here, on the surface, seems to run counter to Luther's Christocentric, grace-focused theology. Luther's opponents were quick to pit James against the Lutheran emphasis on grace. So, Luther said that this epistle is of straw. It lacked Christ, as far as he was concerned. It was not as valuable to his cause as Romans or Galatians.

I have often struggled with this part of Luther. After all, I have been convinced that the entire Scripture comes to us from the Holy Spirit (and I am sure Luther would agree). What this means for me as a pastor is that I am bound to and subject to what the text says in my preaching. All of it. So, if my theology doesn't find James useful, the problem doesn't lie with James but with my system. I decided to put my theology up against James. What I have found is truly wonderful! I believe Luther was wrong (a phrase I will rarely utter!) about James. If we are going to call James an "epistle of straw," then we ought to do so with joy! For in this book, we don't merely have straw but Christ Himself in the straw! I am convinced that we can read James as Luther himself read the Old Testament: "Here you will find the swaddling-clothes and the mangers in which Christ lies, and to which the angel points the shepherds."[2] If James is an "epistle of straw," it is the straw in which we find the dear Jesus, wrapped in swaddling-clothes, laying down for our good!

So, I decided my congregation needed to find Christ in the straw. Though I believe we find Christ all over this book, we also see in James a master preacher

---

2. Luther, "Preface to the Old Testament," in *Basic Theological Writings*, 119.

of the Law. All around, James sees sins that would prevent Christ from being proclaimed and heard. So, James does what any prophet would do when God's gifts are hindered—he attacks with the Law. God's Law—His created will for our lives, which exposes and attacks our sinfulness—is as deadly as it gets in James' letter. But he must attack sin in such a way; otherwise, his hearers would not know their constant need of forgiveness. This book is written to kill the sinner in repentance so that Christ may come in mercy to forgive and raise him or her to a new life—repentance driving us to Christ.

James, it ought to be noted, is also writing to a church that is facing hardship and persecution. This accounts for why his preaching comes across as so harsh. He knows the situation his hearers face does not allow for sweet talk and soft words. The time to repent is now! The time to fight against sin, death, and the devil is now! James knows that the only hope this suffering church has is their Suffering Savior. The church baptized into Christ's death will expect to receive the same reception from the world as their Lord. Yet being united to Christ, we know that no matter what we face, we will be raised in a resurrection like His (Rom. 6:5).

But there are many forces in this world that seek to remove this from us. We need brothers and sisters to call out our sin, to fight alongside us in this world, and to put Christ in our ears. This is the mission of James. "My brothers, if anyone among you wanders from the truth and someone brings him back, let him know that whoever brings back a sinner from his wandering will save his soul from death and will cover a multitude of sins" (Jas. 15:19–20). That, I pray, is what these forty days will do for you.

Each devotion will consist of a short reading from the epistle and a devotional thought. At the end of each day, I have given a prayer for repentance as God's Word in James will convict and kill. This is followed by a daily challenge. The aim here is not to be legalistic but to acknowledge that God's Law both kills and guides. But it can only guide if the person hearing it is born anew in Christ. The Law cannot produce good works; it can only describe them. So, we conclude each devotion with the power of God, the forgiveness of sins. The

Word of absolution both forgives the sinner and raises them to a new life in Christ. We end each day with the Word of mercy, as I believe God's Word of grace is His ultimate Word.

I pray that you will find these devotions to be both challenging and freeing. I pray that through them you will see more clearly the love God has for you in Christ Jesus and the love He has placed in you for your neighbor. Most importantly, I pray that throughout these forty days you will find Christ in the straw and, said even better, He will find you!

Under the Mercy of Christ,
Rev. Bob Hiller

SERVANTS OF JESUS

> *James, a servant of God and of the Lord Jesus Christ, To the twelve tribes scattered among the nations: Greetings.*

James 1:1

I grew up with one brother. If there is a rule that exists between brothers, it is this: defeat the other at all costs. Older brothers must win in whatever battle is being waged, lest they suffer the shame of losing to their *younger* brother. For the younger brother, there is no greater prize than conquering the older. It is constant, intense competition. Loving competition? Sure, I guess, but it is competition, nonetheless. One must never admit defeat!

James, the author of the letter with whom we will be living these next forty days, was the brother of Jesus. And not just in the spiritual sense. It is quite likely that they both had Mary as their mother (though Joseph was not Jesus' father). She certainly raised both of them. Can you imagine what it must have been like for James? Growing up with the perfect, *sinless* Son of God as a brother? You couldn't blame Him for anything, let alone get away with anything! Every "tattle" He told would be the truth! There would be no winning with this one! It would be constant defeat.

5

So, it is rather remarkable to read James' introduction to his epistle: "James, a *servant* of God *and of the Lord Jesus Christ*." He calls himself a servant of the Lord Jesus Christ, his older brother! It is almost as though he is claiming defeat. "He is my Lord; I am His servant. He wins!" But oh, what a joyful defeat!

It is a joyful defeat you've been blessed by as well! In this life, we'll have one of two masters: Satan or Jesus. You are a servant of one or the other. There is no middle ground. You cannot be neutral. You may say, "I am my own master," but that is exactly what Satan would have you say. Anything that gets you away from the gracious rule of Christ is fine by him. His rule is one of sin, pride, accusation, and guilt. His reign leads to death. To be a servant of Satan is to be a slave to sin bound for death.

We are born under such tyranny. But here is the problem: we grow to love it. The darkness becomes comfortable so that when the light of Christ breaks in with the announcement of freedom, we may recoil in fear, perhaps even rebel against the light. Such a rebellion is what put our Liberator on the cross. Our Savior Himself suffered defeat on the cross, but in that defeat, He won victory over sin, death, and Satan! And He did it for you! He rescued the rebels (us) from the wicked slave owner and brought us into the kingdom of His marvelous light, where there is redemption and the forgiveness of sins (Col. 1:13–14).

James, the brother of our Lord, actually encountered Jesus after He had risen from the dead (1 Cor. 15:7). In that encounter, Jesus demonstrated to His brother that He had defeated death and had been given dominion over all creation. James' heart of sin and doubt was replaced with a heart of faith. He was now more than happy to be known as a servant of our Lord and Savior Jesus Christ, his brother. May you know the same joy!

Repent: Heavenly Father, I confess to you that I have not always lived as a servant of your grace. I have tried to be my own lord and run my own life.

I have failed to recognize the authority of your Son over me. Have mercy on me for the sake of His holy death and grant me a spirit of joy in knowing that Christ is my Lord and my brother. AMEN!

Respond: Find a way to show someone in your family that you love them. Write them a note, do a chore for them, or call them up and tell them you love them.

Receive: Jesus Christ is your Lord. But He is a lord who has redeemed you with His blood and rules over you with grace and mercy. His royal declaration for you is this: you are forgiven!

JOY AND TRIALS

> *Consider it pure joy, my brothers, whenever you face trials of many kinds, because you know that the testing of your faith develops perseverance. Perseverance must finish its work so that you may be mature and complete, not lacking anything.*

> **James 1:2–4**

Joy and trials. These are two words you don't typically put together. When I think of trials, I tend to think of long suffering, frustration, endurance, and pain. But joy? Joy is what I feel when I get what I want for Christmas. And you know what I didn't ask for? Trials of any kind.

But notice James does not tell us to feel joy in the midst of our trials, rather, he tells us to consider our trials pure joy. We are to get to know trials in a new way, as joy. How is this possible? James is telling us to look at our trials from a different perspective. We ought to look at our trials from their end point or their goal: perfection in the presence of Christ forever. Our suffering now can be endured with perseverance because we know that our trials are leading to maturity. God is going to take this trial and perfect us through it!

As Christians, we should expect trials of any kind. Though the trials of life test us, God uses them to strengthen our faith. Through His life, Jesus endured many trials. He was tempted by Satan in the desert, attacked for loving and forgiving sinners, betrayed by those He came to save, abandoned by His friends, and ultimately sacrificed for our sins on the cross, where He suffered the wrath of God. His faithful suffering and death led to His resurrection and the salvation of the world. "Therefore God has highly exalted him and bestowed on him the name that is above every name" (Phil. 2:9). Just as Christ was given to endure trials, so too can we expect to face the same. But because Christ endured the trials "for the joy set before Him" (Heb. 12:2), so too can we endure knowing that God will bear us through our trials and raise us on the last day! And that is pure joy!

Repent: Dear Father, I confess that I have a hard time finding joy amid my trials. Grant me the faith and the hope I need to see that you will use my trials to strengthen my faith. I thank you that Jesus suffered for me and promised me eternal joy and that these trials are preparing me for that! AMEN!

Respond: Think of one person outside of the church who is struggling with a trial at this time. Find a way to give them some joy today. Say a prayer for them, buy them coffee, listen to them complain. Whatever you can do to bring some joy to them, do it!

Receive: The Lord Jesus takes great joy and delight in you. He suffered the trial of the cross for the joy set before Him—namely, your salvation! His joy and forgiveness for you will sustain you through your various trials.

FAITH AND DOUBT

> *If any of you lacks wisdom, he should ask God, who gives generously to all without finding fault, and it will be given to him. But when he asks, he must believe and not doubt, because he who doubts is like a wave of the sea, blown and tossed by the wind. That man should not think he will receive anything from the Lord; he is a double-minded man, unstable in all he does.*

James 1:5–8

Yesterday, we heard James teach us that trials are inevitable in the life of the Christian. These trials are used by God to strengthen our faith. But let's be honest: it is hard to trust God in the midst of trials. When suffering and struggling, we find ourselves questioning God and doubting His love for us. We wonder where He is and if He really is working through this trial for us.

In this way, we are much like the apostle Peter when he saw Jesus walking on the water. If you don't know the story, you can read it in Matthew 14:25–33. One night, while sailing through the midst of a storm, the disciples see Jesus walking on the water. It terrifies them! But Jesus speaks words of comfort to them, saying, "Take courage! It is I. Don't be afraid." This calms them all down. But not Peter. He is not convinced. He wants proof and demands as much from Jesus. So, Jesus tells him to get out of the boat and walk to Him on the water. Peter looks to Jesus and starts walking! But when he takes his eyes off of Jesus and focuses on the storm and the waves, he starts sinking. In his doubt, Peter finds himself being "blown and tossed by the wind." He is drowning in his doubt.

During our trials, the danger is not so much the trial itself but where we fix our eyes. We are either listening to the wind and the waves or listening to the words of Jesus: "Take courage! It is I. Don't be afraid." There is great comfort in noticing where Jesus stood while Peter was afraid: He stood above Peter, picking him up and putting him back in the boat. Jesus doesn't leave us in our trials. The trials are real; the wind and the waves are strong. But the Jesus who walks on water will never leave us nor forsake us. He's always there, pulling us out of the water and bringing us back to the boat.

Repent: Lord God, I admit to you now that I do not fully trust you as I should. Like Peter, I find myself doubting your love, mercy, and presence. Amid my trials, I focus more on the storm than your Son. In your mercy, pull me out of the water, forgive my sins, and place me in the boat of your security. AMEN!

Respond: Find someone you know who is facing a trial or struggle right now. Pray with them or for them as a reminder to them that the Lord is with them. Next week, follow up on the prayer you prayed.

Receive: The Lord never left Peter, even when Peter turned away. In the waters of your baptism, Christ Jesus has promised to save you and will not turn away from His promises. His baptismal promises stand firm especially when your faith is weak. He promises you are forgiven.

FADING RICHES

> *The brother in humble circumstances ought to take pride in his high position. But the one who is rich should take pride in his low position, because he will pass away like a wild flower. For the sun rises with scorching heat and withers the plant; its blossom falls and its beauty is destroyed. In the same way, the rich man will fade away even while he goes about his business.*

James 1:9–11

The church James is writing to is facing persecution. These were people who had no need to practice a Lenten fast or self-imposed suffering because their livelihood had likely been taken from them for confessing their faith in Jesus. By simply claiming Jesus as Lord and God, these people risked losing house and home. Those who were wealthy risked losing their financial security.

In the face of such a possibility, it seems the wealthy may have been considering avoiding persecution in favor of keeping their livelihood. The reality was that money was their god, and they were prepared to choose worldly wealth over persecution for their faith! They loved money and security more than Jesus!

13

James gives us a stark contrast here between the exalted poor and the humbled rich. In the kingdom of heaven, it is better to be poor and persecuted for the name of Jesus than it is to be wealthy, comfortable, and faithless in the world. The least in the eyes of the world—the brother or sister who is poor but has Christ—has great cause to rejoice, for they are first in the kingdom of heaven (Matt. 19:28–30)! Wealth is fleeting, and it matters precious little on the day of judgment.

If we are honest, we will admit that the prospect of losing our position, status, or comfort terrifies us. Who of us wouldn't struggle to stand by Jesus if it meant losing our lifestyle? Yet this is a reality that many Christians do face in our world today and one we may also have to deal with one day. When such temptations to wealth over Jesus arise, we must cling to the promises of heaven God makes to those in humble circumstances. We must remember our Lord Jesus, who for our sake became poor, hung as the least of all on the cross, so that we would be exalted with Him forever.

Repent: Almighty Father, I confess to you that my love for wealth and comfort very often trumps my love for you and your kingdom. I honestly do not know how I would respond in the face of persecution. I praise you for your Son who endured humiliation on my behalf. Grant me the same Holy Spirit who gave Jesus the resolve in the face of the cross. Make me steadfast unto the day of resurrection. AMEN!

Respond: St. Paul tells Pastor Timothy to exhort the wealthy to "be rich in good deeds, and to be generous and willing to share." By yourself or with your family, pray about and begin searching for a ministry that supports persecuted Christians. Find ways you can help them in their efforts.

Receive: Jesus did not place value in the things this world finds valuable. Instead, He left His throne in heaven and chose to reign from a cross because He loves you. He died so you would live. He was cursed so you would be forgiven. You are treasured by the Lord Himself!

TEMPTATION

> *Blessed is the man who perseveres under trial, because when he has stood the test, he will receive the crown of life that God has promised to those who love him. When tempted, no one should say, "God is tempting me." For God cannot be tempted by evil, nor does he tempt anyone; but each one is tempted when, by his own evil desire, he is dragged away and enticed. Then, after desire has conceived, it gives birth to sin; and sin, when it is full-grown, gives birth to death. Don't be deceived, my dear brothers.*

James 1:12–16

"The devil made me do it!" Have you ever thought this when you've been caught sinning? We are all too ready to play the victim card when we are caught up in sins and trials. Some go so far as to blame God for temptations they face, justifying their actions with foolish thoughts like, "Well, if God didn't want me to commit this sin, He wouldn't have allowed the opportunity to arise" or "God made me this way, so how I feel cannot be wrong." But James is very clear to us today: sin comes from inside of us. It is our fault. Our own "evil desires" are all too ready to answer the sweet, deceptive call of temptation.

Temptations are trials that sinners will inevitably face. Christian sinners will especially be attacked. Though we fight and struggle, far too often, we give in to the trials that seek to draw us away from Christ. As we have seen, the church to which James is writing is being tempted to abandon Jesus so as to avoid persecution. Though our physical lives may not be at stake when we are tempted, every temptation is an enticement of Satan to drag us away from our Savior. How can we hope to endure difficult trials and receive the crown of life when we find ourselves so weak?

Psalm 1 says that one whose delight is in God's Word is blessed: "He is like a tree planted by streams of water, which yields its fruit in season and whose leave does not wither. Whatever he does prospers" (Ps. 1:3). In the midst of the temptations that scorch us like the desert sun, Christ's Word comes as refreshing water that refreshes us and strengthens us to face the trials in our lives. It is the Word that says Jesus has endured the trial of the cross to forgive our sinful weakness, or as James calls it, our evil desires. It is the Word that tells us that God has raised Jesus from the dead and "crowned" Him with authority over all creation, and He rules over you in love and mercy. To cease from hearing this Word is to venture into the desert of temptation without water. But to regularly hear this Word in worship is to be planted next to the life-giving streams and receive refreshing from the One who has conquered your temptations.

Repent: O gracious God, who blesses parched sinners with the refreshing water of your Gospel, forgive me, for I have given into temptation. I have prayed that you would not lead me into temptation, and yet I confess to you that I have put myself in places that appeal to my evil desires. For the sake of your Son's blood, give me perseverance in the face of trials so that I will receive the gracious crown you promise your people. AMEN.

Respond: Today's challenge will be one that leads to repentance. Take the Ten Commandments and read through them. Write down which of these you are most tempted to break. Pray that the Lord would give you forgiveness for your sins and seek ideas in how you can fight against this sin. (A Small Catechism will prove helpful in this challenge.)

Receive: On Sunday morning, in many churches, the pastor will announce the grace of God to you and say, "I forgive your sins in the name of the Father and the Son and the Holy Spirit." That is the pastor's voice, but it is Jesus' Word he speaks. That is Christ's forgiveness that crowns you and grounds you in His love.

GOOD GIFTS

> *Every good and perfect gift is from above, coming down from the Father of the heavenly lights, who does not change like shifting shadows. He chose to give us birth through the word of truth, that we might be a kind of firstfruits of all he created.*

James 1:17–18

In the midst of trials and temptations, it is hard to remember that God is our Father who gives all good gifts! In the midst of trial and temptation, suffering and persecution, our faith may waiver. As the band Caedmon's Call sings in their song "Shifting Sand," "My faith is like shifting sand, changed by every wave." Like a boat on the waves, our faith is up and down. At times, we feel like we are thriving, and other times, we feel like we are failing. The song goes on, "My faith is like shifting sand, so I stand on grace!" Our faith may shift, but God does not "change like the shifting shadows!" He remains the God of good gifts.

Every good gift comes from above, James says. That is the movement in our relationship with God: from God to us. In the incarnation, God *gives* Jesus to us in human flesh to preach His saving message. On the cross, Jesus *gives* up His life as a sacrifice for our sins. He *gives* Himself to God for us. Because Christ has done this, the Father *gives* us new birth in baptism by giving us the Holy Spirit through the Word of truth. He *gives* us His body and blood in bread and wine at the Lord's Supper as a forgiving gift. He *gives* us a new life so that even our Christian living is a gift from Him!

The entire life of a Christian—new birth and maturation, justification and sanctification, the promise of resurrection beyond trials—all of it is a gift from God. All of it is ours because of the greatest gift God has given us: His one and only Son, Jesus Christ. Jesus is the gift of the Father and the giver of salvation. God is a giver, and that never changes!

Repent: Dear Father, all good gifts come from you. I confess that I have neglected your Son and not lived the life of faith you have given to me. Forgive me for the sake of Jesus and strengthen me to receive your gifts with faith and joy! AMEN!

Respond: Go to a coffee shop, restaurant, or someplace where you must stand in line for food and pay for the person behind you in line as a pure gift.

Receive: Faith is a gift that receives the gift of salvation. So open wide your hands, and Christ will fill them with this promise: You are forgiven. He is the giver, and you are free to enjoy the gift!

QUICK TO LISTEN, SLOW TO SPEAK

> *My dear brothers, take note of this: Everyone should be quick to listen, slow to speak and slow to become angry, for man's anger does not bring about the righteous life that God desires. Therefore, get rid of all moral filth and the evil that is so prevalent and humbly accept the word planted in you, which can save you.*

James 1:19–21

Read this text again closely. Ask yourself this question: Are you quick to listen or quick to speak? When you are having an argument or are in a debate with someone, do you take the time to listen to the other person's side, or are you trying to win for the sake of being right? We are always ready to prove ourselves right at the cost of someone else's pride. This is the world's way of arguing—win at all costs!

But in baptism, Jesus has placed His Word in us so that we are no longer "of the world" (John 17:16). We have a God who has spoken a different Word to us. James says He has planted it in us! This Word is Jesus Himself! Jesus, our God, forgives our sins and trespasses. Jesus, our God, does not seek to belittle us with His righteousness but seeks to clothe us in it. His Word of forgiveness and grace actually brings about the righteous life that God desires. We are to be quick to listen to God's Word so that it shapes the way we speak and act.

We should not be impressed by quick-witted talking heads who make their opponents look like fools. We have been born to a new life, which is shaped by God's Word of grace. The way we speak is a reflection and outgrowth of the Word God has spoken to us. Words of grace find themselves on our lips as the Spirit works through the Word implanted in our hearts. "For God, who said, 'Let light shine out of darkness,' made his light shine in our hearts to give us the light of the knowledge of the glory of God in the face of Christ" (2 Cor. 4:6).

Repent: Father of all mercies, by your mighty Word, you created this world, and by that same gracious Word, you have created a new heart within me. Forgive me when my words do not echo your Words. I confess that I care more about being right than loving my neighbor. Forgive me and use my mouth to declare your praise. AMEN!

Respond: Next time you are in an argument, lose.

Receive: Jesus did not seek to win you by exalting Himself to your shame. Instead, He set aside His glory, took on the form of a servant, and sacrificed everything for your salvation. He does not use His Words to shame you to His own glory, but rather, it is His glory to speak Words of mercy, forgiveness, and healing to you. You are forgiven and beloved, He said so!

DO WHAT IT SAYS!

> *Do not merely listen to the word, and so deceive yourselves. Do what it says. Anyone who listens to the word but does not do what it says is like a man who looks at his face in a mirror and, after looking at himself, goes away and immediately forgets what he looks like. But the man who looks intently into the perfect law that gives freedom, and continues to do this, not forgetting what he has heard, but doing it—he will be blessed in what he does.*

James 1:22–25

The Law that gives freedom? What is James talking about? After all, isn't the Law that Word from God that reveals our sin to us? Isn't it the Law that condemns sinners? The Law cannot free us; it is by its very nature a slave driver! How can James tell us to look intently to the Law that gives freedom?

It must be remembered that the Law of God is always at work in three ways. First, it is warning us that, if we break it, there will be penalties to pay. For fear of punishment, we try to keep the Law. For example, the law says, "Don't speed, or else you will get a ticket." So, we don't speed to avoid the ticket. God says, "If you obey my commands perfectly, you will live. If not, you will die. Eternally." Second, then, the law always, *always*, accuses us because we know that we have sped! We have broken the Law by sinning against God's commands. The Law crushes us and kills us because we know that we cannot live by keeping it. Here, the Law reveals to us our need for Christ and, in a sense, serves the Gospel as it causes us to despair of our righteousness and goodness and to cry out to God for mercy.

God's answer to the Law, and to our cries, is Jesus. Jesus kept the Law on our behalf, perfectly, so that, according to the Law, He did not have to die. So that, when He does die, it is on your behalf, taking your sin, your guilt, and the punishments of the Law away from you onto Himself. Here, we are set free from having to obey the Law for our salvation!

Now we are free! But here is the ironic part: we are free to keep the Law! What does that mean? It means that since the Law no longer condemns us, we no longer have to fear it. Instead, the third way God uses the Law is as a guide to show us how to live in the freedom of the Gospel toward our neighbor. We look to the Law to see how it is we *can* live as those who have been given a new life of freedom in Christ Jesus. We are not free *to* sin (that would be a return to slavery); we are free *from* sin and therefore free from the condemnations of the Law. We can look at the Law to see who we are in Christ Jesus. We can see it as a description of how our lives can now be lived. We don't just hear what we are to be; rather, by being possessions of the Holy Spirit, we actually live it out! We are freed to do what it says without fear!

Repent: Mighty and gracious Lord, have mercy on me. I confess that I have despised your Law. I have even used your promises of forgiveness as an excuse to break your Law. I have abused your grace. I plead before you, for the sake of your Son's holy, innocent, and bitter suffering to have mercy on me, a sinner. Graciously grant me your Holy Spirit so that I might live my life according to your will. AMEN!

Respond: Find a Small Catechism and memorize one commandment and its explanation. Pray for an opportunity to act on this commandment this week.

Receive: Though you are free from the Law's condemnation (Rom. 8:1), you probably still feel its accusations. Fear not! Jesus has kept the Law for you, and He gives you credit for His work! When the accusations weigh heavy on you, send the Law to Jesus. He has and will take care of it for you!

ACCEPTABLE RELIGION

> *If anyone considers himself religious and yet does not keep a tight rein on his tongue, he deceives himself and his religion is worthless. Religion that God our Father accepts as pure and faultless is this: to look after orphans and widows in their distress and to keep oneself from being polluted by the world.*

James 1:26–27

"Religion" seems to be a bad word in the culture these days. Some Christians have even tried to distance themselves from it. People say they love Jesus but hate religion. Or they will say that Christianity is about a relationship, not about religion. When people talk this way, they are probably thinking of religion as rules, regulations, and rituals that must be obeyed if one wants to be right with God. In other words, religions are those legalistic systems that are set up to earn a spot in heaven. They are judgmental and oppressive toward those who don't fit in with their standards and laws. Thus "religion" is a bad word.

Not all religion is bad, however. In fact, James rescues us from such a false view of religion today by pointing us to what it looks like to be a part of a religion that is shaped by Jesus. Jesus Himself builds His church and shapes the life of that church by His own life, death, and resurrection. Jesus, the founder of our religion, gives us an entirely different sort of religion because He is a different sort of Lord! He's the sort that serves us who are poor, broken, distraught, or oppressed by sins and life's circumstances. He's the sort who enters into our suffering in His incarnation and pays our debt to God in His crucifixion. The Lord of our religion gives all He has on behalf of those who are in distress.

Our God is a God who looks after His people. He cares for those who are broken by the world by sending His Son to bear the load of the world. This Son makes us acceptable to God. Our religion—that is, our life as believers in this God—is now shaped by the God who looks after us. Therefore, we look after others who are poor, broken, and weak. We care for those who are unable to care for themselves. The widows and orphans in James' day had no means of providing for themselves so it was on the church to provide for them. How can we as the church look out for those in need? Who are the orphans and widows around us that the Lord would call us to look after?

Repent: Dear Father of my faith, have mercy on me. I confess that I have spoken loudly about my religion but have not acted in accordance with my words. I am weak in good works. For the sake of your Son, who has saved me from the poverty of sin, forgive me. Renew me so that I would reflect the love of Christ toward those I know who are in need of Christ's love. AMEN!

Respond: Help someone around you who is in need. The need doesn't have to be great. You could just run an errand for someone at work. Or you could go big and take a homeless person out to lunch. The sky is the limit!

Receive: James tells us true religion looks after widows and orphans. This is because our religion reflects the God who looks out for the needy. Your sins have rendered you in need of forgiveness and salvation. Thus Jesus has come for you! Your need is met by Jesus your Savior, who declares your sins forgiven!

FAVORITISM

> *My brothers, as believers in our glorious Lord Jesus Christ, don't show favoritism. Suppose a man comes into your meeting wearing a gold ring and fine clothes, and a poor man in shabby clothes also comes in. If you show special attention to the man wearing fine clothes and say, "Here's a good seat for you," but say to the poor man, "You stand there" or "Sit on the floor by my feet," have you not discriminated among yourselves and become judges with evil thoughts?*

James 2:1–4

Favoritism. The word just sends shivers down my spine! I break out in a cold sweat just picturing those torturous days in junior high school: not being welcome to sit at the "popular" table, being excluded from games on the playground, not having partners for class projects. Oh, the horror! Remember how this went with us into high school? The effort we all put into finding our "clique." Finding value in who your friends are is difficult. Especially when your "clique" is not the popular one!

At least for me, trying to fit in was one of the worst parts about growing up. I can imagine we all have clique-related horror stories. But if cliques were so horrible growing up, why do we find them appearing in the church? Of all the places where such attitudes should not exist, the church should be the chief. Yet somehow, holy friendships turn into popularity alliances. We find ourselves gradually moving toward those who are most like us, have shared interests with us, or, at our worst moments, are of the greatest advantage to us in our lives.

James is writing to a congregation where the rich are considered more blessed by God than the poor. So, they are given better seats in church, shown more respect, and granted prominence. All the while, the poor are made to stand off to the side. In a world of celebrity worship, it is not hard to picture the scene: a famous person walks into church and the noisy children are told to move so that our idol can have a better seat!

James says this must not be! We are believers in Jesus Christ, who Himself became poor and lowly and spent His time with the unpopular crowd. He spent time with those who were otherwise ostracized from society. What is more, He healed them, restored them, and forgave them. He was (and is) exalting them so that He could say, "Blessed are the poor in spirit, for theirs is the kingdom of heaven" (Matt. 5:3).

We must be reminded that no one is more important in church than anyone else. We are all one in Christ Jesus. Baptism is the great equalizer, where we are reminded that we have all received the same Lord and the same salvation, for we are all similarly sinful and in need of God's gracious work in Jesus (Gal. 3:26–29; Eph. 4:3–6).

It is my prayer that we can come to church without the fear of cliques. Instead, when we walk in the doors of our church, we can embrace each and every person in the sanctuary and join hands in singing to our one God who has saved each of us by His grace!

Repent: God of all grace and mercy, in the waters of baptism, you have chosen me to be your child, and you have included me in your family. Forgive me for the times when I have excluded or avoided my brothers and sisters in our fellowship. Thank you for including me in this family and grant me the strength to love all the baptized with the love you have given me. AMEN!

Respond: Next Sunday, find someone at church you've never spoken to before and introduce yourself. If you know everyone, sit next to someone you don't normally sit next to.

Receive: Jesus loves and welcomes sinners who do not deserve His love. He removes whatever it is that would keep them away from the table of the Lord and welcomes them to the feast. Never forget, you are that sinner! He has a place for you! No matter how the world has treated you, no matter how the church has treated you, the Dear Lord is thrilled to have brought you into His presence!

CHOOSING THE POOR

> *Listen, my dear brothers: Has not God chosen those who are poor in the eyes of the world to be rich in faith and to inherit the kingdom he promised those who love him? But you have insulted the poor. Is it not the rich who are exploiting you? Are they not the ones who are dragging you into court? Are they not the ones who are slandering the noble name of him to whom you belong?*

James 2:5–7

I recently heard about a sermon a friend of mine preached at the congregation where I served as a vicar (i.e., as an intern pastor). Just before the service started, a homeless-looking man walked into the large sanctuary and sat right in the midst of the well-kept congregants. He smelled bad. He was constantly making little noises. During the service, he took out a sandwich and started eating. As the service progressed, those sitting in his vicinity slowly and slyly moved away. By the time the sermon began, the man was sitting by himself. The pastor then began to preach on how we treat those who come into our church and make us uncomfortable. The "homeless" man was actually a local actor hired by the pastor to prove a point. And it worked.

In our world, we tend to categorize people in order to keep ourselves safe. We stay away from those who fall in a different category from us. In fact, we'll even demonize those in other categories just to justify our avoidance of them. We'll leave the poor on their side of town and only associate with those who are in a similar socioeconomic category as us. For as loving as we like to think we are, we still avoid certain neighborhoods with "those" kinds of people. We stay on our side of the tracks.

Such a worldly attitude has no place in the church. Our God, after all, has chosen the poor in the eyes of the world to be rich in faith! Faith is true wealth. To try to turn the church into a place where the rich are honored and the poor are marginalized is to deny baptism or, as James says, to slander the noble name of Him to whom you belong. We all share a common baptism where we are all marked with the name of the triune God. We are all made coheirs with Christ. Here, in Christ, there is neither Jew nor Greek, slave nor free, male nor female, for we are all one in Christ Jesus (Gal. 3:28). To insult the poor is to insult the One who baptized the poor alongside you. Here, social status means nothing. Christ is everything.

Repent: Heavenly Father, I praise you that you have placed your name on me in the waters of baptism and united me to your family, the church. I confess, however, that I have looked down on my brothers and sisters for proud and self-righteous reasons. I have not loved my neighbor as myself, and therefore, have not loved you with my whole heart. Keep me in my baptismal grace, forgive me for my pride, and teach me to love all my brothers and sisters just as you have loved me in my poverty. AMEN.

Respond: Write a note to someone at church (besides the pastor) whose work you appreciate. Thank them for their hard work.

Receive: The Lord Jesus looks on you in the same way He looks on every other weak, poor, and lowly sinner—with mercy. He became poor, bled, suffered, and died so that He might purchase you with His precious blood and shower you in the riches of His grace. No matter how poor or wealthy you are in this world, in Christ Jesus you are rich!

THE WHOLE LAW

> *If you really keep the royal law found in Scripture, "Love your neighbor as yourself," you are doing right. But if you show favoritism, you sin and are convicted by the law as lawbreakers. For whoever keeps the whole law and yet stumbles at just one point is guilty of breaking all of it. For he who said, "Do not commit adultery," also said, "Do not murder." If you do not commit adultery but do commit murder, you have become a lawbreaker.*

James 2:8–11

We have a great way of downplaying our sin. We will call our sins "mistakes" or "accidents." We tend to view some sins as worse than others. Conveniently, the sins we see as being the worst are the ones "they" are committing. We say, "Not me! My sins aren't that bad; they are just mistakes." James has no time for such word games. Stumbling against God's law at just one point—one measly, little point—makes you a lawbreaker. You who stumble are guilty of breaking the whole thing. Period.

Thus far in this chapter, James has focused on the sin of favoritism. He says it breaks the Law of God. We may well ask, what is the Law that is broken? I don't recall any of the commandments saying, "Thou shall not show favoritism." So how can James tell me I am a lawbreaker here if that law isn't exactly one of the top ten?

To show favoritism doesn't just break one law; it is to break commandments four through ten, summarized in the royal law, "Love your neighbor as yourself!" These commandments teach us how God wants us to treat others. Yet favoritism is always selfish because with it we are always favoring ourselves. We show favoritism when we think we can get something out of someone else. Think about it: Why are the rich exalted over the poor? Because they are better people? No! But because we can get something out of them. We use them for our own ends. It is the same with the example James gives of adultery. No one commits adultery because they love someone; they do it because it makes them feel good, alive, young, free, or something stupid like that.

Favoritism is self-love. Self-love breaks the commands of God. Breaking the commands of God means placing yourself above God. Every sin says, "I know better than He what I should be doing with my life." Thus, every sin committed is a breaking of the first commandment: "You shall have no other gods before me" (Ex. 20:3). We are putting ourselves before God, thus making ourselves out to be our own gods.

Our sins are deadly. They are the evidence that our hearts are not as right as we think they are. Such a realization sends us fleeing to the cross for mercy. Christ does not come to help guide those who make mistakes to make better choices. He comes to forgive sinners. Though He never broke the Law once, He comes to stand as though He was the chief lawbreaker before God on behalf of the true lawbreaker—you! He takes your place. If our sins are small, why is God hanging on a cross? Fellow lawbreaker, you are forgiven for His sake because He was the sin bearer on your behalf.

Repent: God of all mercy, I cannot come into your presence on my own, for I am a lawbreaker who has transgressed your holiness. I have favored myself over you and your people. I have lived as if I mattered most, without love for others or you. I deserve death, the penalty for breaking your law. I praise you that Jesus has taken my death for me. I pray that because of your infinite mercy and for the sake of your Son's holy, innocent, and bitter sufferings, you would forgive and renew me to love you with my whole heart and my neighbor as myself. AMEN!

Respond: Revisit the commandment you were supposed to memorize a few days ago. Have you had a chance to act on it? How did it go? Continue to work on that today.

Receive: Though being in very nature God, Jesus did not consider equality with God a thing to be grasped but took on the form of a servant so that He would offer up His life as a sacrifice for you! You, a lawbreaker, have a Savior who places your salvation above His own good and sacrificed everything to forgive and save you. And now, He's your Lord who rules over you with the promise "I forgive you!" and with nothing but your salvation as His goal.

JUDGMENT AND MERCY

> *Speak and act as those who are going to be judged by the law that gives freedom, because judgment without mercy will be shown to anyone who has not been merciful. Mercy triumphs over judgment!*

James 2:12–13

Mercy is everything for the Christian. Mercy for the sake of Christ's death is the basis and the sustaining principle in our relationship with our Heavenly Father. Mercy is the language of repentance and prayer: "Lord, have mercy!" Mercy not only characterizes God's love toward His children; it also forms the lives of His children in their relationships with one another. We are a people of mercy.

But what if it is otherwise? What if the children of God begin to take His mercy for granted and start to withhold mercy from one another? In Matthew 18:23–35, Jesus tells a parable about a servant who was forgiven an enormous debt by a gracious king. The debt was too large and so he begged the king for mercy. The king gave it and graciously forgave the debt. Later that day the servant went out and found someone who owed him a couple of bucks. He began choking the man, demanding his money. The man with the small debt fell to his knees and begged the servant to have patience, he would pay him back. The servant refused and threw the man in jail. Hearing the news about the servant, the king, in his anger, threw the wicked servant back in jail to be tortured until he could pay back everything.

God is eternally and incredibly merciful. He has canceled the debt of your sin with the blood of Jesus. He has forgiven you and set you free from con- demnation under the Law. But too often we use His mercy as an excuse to sin: "I don't need to forgive that person who has hurt me so much. God will forgive me no matter what." If there is one thing we must never say about God's mercy, it is that it is an excuse for us to withhold forgiveness and mercy toward those who have wronged us. God's mercy triumphs over judgment; it doesn't excuse it.

Repent: Heavenly Father, I fall on my knees before you and plead for your great mercy. I beg you for the sake of your Son Jesus, whose death has removed my great debt of sin, to forgive me for my lack of mercy. As I leave this time of confession today, do not let me be like the servant in Jesus' parable who used his freedom to condemn his brother. Rather, teach me to forgive others, just as you have forgiven me. In Jesus' name, I pray, AMEN.

Respond: Forgive someone who has wronged you. If you cannot do this, repent again, and beg the Lord to give you a heart of mercy.

Receive: The debt you owe God is far more immense than you could ever imagine. The price to pay for your sins would mean eternal death for you. But one drop of the blood of Jesus is worth far more than your sin, and it is with that blood that He pays the debt you owe. You are free. You owe noth- ing. Your debts are forgiven.

DEAD FAITH, PART 1

> *What good is it, my brothers, if a man claims to have faith but has no deeds? Can such faith save him? Suppose a brother or sister is without clothes and daily food. If one of you says to him, "Go, I wish you well; keep warm and well fed," but does nothing about his physical needs, what good is it? In the same way, faith by itself, if it is not accompanied by action, is dead.*

James 2:14–17

Can a faith that has no deeds be a saving faith? This is the question that will engage us for the next few days of our study. We work very hard to teach that faith alone, apart from works, saves a Christian. We won't do enough to save ourselves nor can we. Our sin is too great. So, Christ comes purely and solely by God's grace to save us. He does not look to see if we are holy enough or if we are worthy enough. God saves sinners by grace alone through faith alone on account of Christ alone. It is faith alone in Jesus, apart from works, that saves you (Eph. 2:8–9).

James is not disagreeing with this truth today. James wants to emphasize that, though faith alone does save us, saving faith is never alone. In other words, Jesus saves us, not our works. But faith in Jesus is never without works of love for the neighbor. Faith is always working, always loving. The question is not "Can a faith with no deeds be a saving faith?" Rather, the question is "Can a saving faith have no deeds?" or "Is it even possible for saving faith to not be working?"

Martin Luther said it this way:

> **Faith is a divine [that is to say, God's] work in us and makes us to be born anew of God. It kills the old 'Adam' and makes us altogether different people, in heart and spirit and mind and all powers; and it brings with it the Holy Spirit. O, it is a living, busy, active, mighty thing, this faith. It is impossible for it not to be doing good works incessantly . . . Thus, it is impossible to separate works from faith, quite as impossible as to separate heat and light from fire. (LW 35:370–371)**

Faith is loving all the time. Faith trusts God for all things and loves the neighbor with all things. It is not this love that saves us, but it is love that comes from those who are saved by God's grace. If such love is absent, the question becomes "Does faith even exist?"

Consider Luther's illustration of the heat and light that come from fire. If I took you into a cold, dark room and said, "Look at how beautiful that fire is! Isn't it magnificent?" you would look at me like I was crazy. The room is clearly without fire because there is no heat and no light, which always come from fire. So it is with faith. James says that if we go about boasting of our great faith but do not love our brothers and sisters in the church, then we are boasting of a great fire in a cold, dark room. If there are those among us who are poor, hungry, and naked and we say, "I hope that works out for you. Oh, I'll pray for you," and leave them poor, hungry, and naked our faith looks to be dead. God has graciously saved us poor, wretched sinners out of the abundance of His mercy and grace. Faith trusts this promise for salvation. That faith saves. But that faith also works. It loves just as God has loved us.

Repent: Gracious, Heavenly Father, have mercy on me for the sake of your Son, Jesus Christ. I confess how much I struggle to exercise my faith in love toward those around me. I love my things and my comfort so much that I don't share with those in need. You have given me faith in Jesus; now give me an active love for my neighbor. AMEN!

Respond: Next time you offer to pray for someone who is hurting, don't wait to pray. Pray for them there on the spot. Then offer to help them with their problem in a real, concrete way.

Receive: Jesus has called you to love your neighbor as yourself. But know this: He has loved you first. He has called you to sacrifice for those in need. He offered His life as a sacrifice for your need of forgiveness and salvation. Your sin left you naked and hungry. Jesus has clothed you with His righteousness and now feeds you with His body and blood in the sacrament.

DEAD FAITH, PART 2

> *But someone will say, "You have faith; I have deeds." Show me your faith without deeds, and I will show you my faith by what I do. You believe that there is one God. Good! Even the demons believe that—and shudder.*

James 2:18–19

Yesterday, we learned that faith alone in Christ saves us but that faith is never alone. It is always active in love. At this point, it may seem as if James wants only to talk about works. But on closer examination of the reading, it would seem that James is primarily concerned about faith! The issue of works comes up here because those who claim to have faith have no works to prove it. It is great that folks show up to church and confess the creed and say they believe there is one God. The demons have that knowledge too. But faith is not merely a matter of knowing facts. It is a matter of believing promises. Such belief is evident in the way Christians live.

Here is an example of what I mean: Every Christian will readily say that they believe it is God who provides them with their daily bread. We pray for it in the Lord's Prayer and believe that God answers that prayer faithfully, right?

We say we believe that, but then how do we live? Do we give of our means as if we believe God will provide for us again the next day? When it comes to giving offerings to the church or helping the poor, how much do you give? Do you give in a way that stings a little? Or do you throw a couple bucks their way, knowing it will ease your conscience? Does the way we give reflect our confession that God will give us daily bread? It's like telling your spouse you love them but doing everything you can to ignore them. Inactive love is not love.

Perhaps the problem is that our faith is not nearly as strong as we think it is and so we hold back from love and risk. It is the old sinful nature that doesn't believe God will do what He said. We do the same thing with salvation. We confess that salvation is a gift from Jesus and there is nothing left to do to be saved but then we come up with all kinds of legalistic practices to make sure we are in. Typically, those practices are very self-serving with no regard for the neighbor. We do good things not to demonstrate love but to make ourselves feel saved.

Faith is not knowledge of mere facts. Faith is not merely knowing who God is and what He has done. It is believing that He has done it *for you*. The demons fear Jesus and want to flee from Him (Mark 1:24). But faith believes that Jesus has come for you, to love you and grant you all things by His grace. Such certainty, wrought by the Holy Spirit, enables and empowers us to act on our faith in love, knowing that we have all things in Christ and Christ has us.

Repent: Merciful Father, I believe that you have loved me with an everlasting love because Jesus shed His blood for me. But I confess that at times my faith is found lacking. I cling to the securities of this life more than the promises you make. Forgive me, dear Lord. Do not permit me to have a mere knowledge of the truth but teach me to trust the truth and live in accordance with it. I ask this in Jesus' name. AMEN!

Respond: Write a check to a mission, ministry, or even your church this Sunday for an amount that makes you uncomfortable.

Receive: James shows again and again that faith proves itself in the activities of love. This sort of faith is given by a God who demonstrates His love for you in the most marvelous of actions: sending His Son Jesus to die for you while you were yet a sinner. You are forgiven because God has acted for you in Christ.

DEAD FAITH, PART 3

> *You foolish man, do you want evidence that faith without deeds is useless? Was not our ancestor Abraham considered righteous for what he did when he offered his son Isaac on the altar? You see that his faith and his actions were working together, and his faith was made complete by what he did. And the scripture was fulfilled that says, "Abraham believed God, and it was credited to him as righteousness," and he was called God's friend. You see that a person is justified by what he does and not by faith alone.*
>
> **James 2:20–24**

"Aha! I knew it," you say. "I knew it was too good to be true: all this saved-by-faith-alone-apart-from-works business. There it is, plain as day; James says it: we are justified by what we do and not faith alone!" Could it be? Have we been wrong about the free gift of salvation all along? Do we really have to work in order to be justified before God? Are we saved by grace plus works? Or is something else going on here?

How are we to understand this along with what St. Paul says, for example, in Galatians 2:16? "[We] know that a man is *not* justified by observing the law, *but by faith* in Jesus Christ. So we, too, have put our faith in Christ Jesus that we may be *justified by faith* in Christ and *not by observing the law*, because *by observing the law no one will be justified*" (emphasis mine; see also Rom. 5:28 and Eph. 2:8–10). Which is it? Are we justified by observing the Law (what we do) or by faith alone in what Jesus has done? Is it James or Paul?

Before we all flee from the "faith-alone" church to one teaching "works righteousness," it is worth our time to review what has gone on so far in this chapter. (Take a moment to reread 2:1–19.) As we have seen, James is addressing a group of Christians who apparently do not believe they have to be a reflection of God's love. They got their salvation for free, and since they didn't have to do anything to get it, they believe they no longer have to do anything in light of it. This is dead faith. This is to remain in slavery to sin. The Gospel is not an excuse to disobey God's Law; rather, it frees us from *the condemnation* of the Law so we can freely live according to the Law, without fear of condemnation (see Rom. 8:1). That is what faith does, and if your faith isn't doing that, James says, you are not saved. Wow!

Both Paul and James are saying the same thing. Context is critical here. Paul is addressing Christians who believe there is something they must add to their salvation. These are people who don't believe Jesus is sufficient for salvation. So, Paul tells them, Jesus is all you need. Don't trust your obedience to God's Law, trust Jesus. It is faith alone. James agrees that it is faith alone that saves us. But he is addressing people with the opposite problem. They are abusing the truth of faith alone as an excuse to not love God and neighbor. So, he must remind them (and us!) in the starkest of terms that faith is never alone. It is always working in love. In this sense, "alone faith" cannot justify because faith without love is dead faith. As Paul himself says in 1 Corinthians 13:2, "If I have the faith that can move mountains, but do not have love, I am nothing."

Salvation is a free gift from God to sinners. Faith alone in Christ alone because of God's grace alone saves you. Salvation is all His doing. And when

He saves you, He gives you one very active Holy Spirit to produce fruit in your life! This is busy, active faith indeed! Faith alone saves you. But saving, living faith is never alone.

Repent: Heavenly Father, I confess that I have used your grace as an excuse to sin. I have tried to make myself feel better for sinning by saying, "Well, at least I have faith." Forgive me for not expressing my faith in love. Forgive me for not reflecting your love for me. Grant to me a heart of active faith. AMEN!

Respond: Consider offering to clean up around your church one Saturday. Bring your family or organize a group to take care of the church property.

Receive: Just as faith is never without works, God's promises are never without gifts. He has given you His salvation in baptism, He has given you His promise in the absolution, and He has given you His body and blood in the bread and wine at the Lord's Supper. The God who sends you to act for others works for you in the sacrament.

LIVING FAITH

> *In the same way, was not even Rahab the prostitute considered righteous for what she did when she gave lodging to the spies and sent them off in a different direction? As the body without the spirit is dead, so faith without deeds is dead.*
>
> **James 2:25–26**

These last few days, James has made it abundantly clear that when it comes to how Christians live their lives, faith is not an excuse to abandon love. Faith without works is dead. In a shocking illustration, he compares a loveless faith to a dead body. It just isn't doing anything. Quite frankly, if you let it stay around too long, it becomes disgusting.

So, are you getting the picture of how our Lord feels about loveless faith? I hope so. James is good to us today, then, by giving us a beautiful example of what an active faith looks like in the person of Rahab the prostitute. You may not be familiar with her story, so I suggest reading Joshua 2:1–24. The Israelites are about to enter the Promised Land, but many of God's enemies stand in their way. Among those enemies are the inhabitants of Jericho. When the Israelite spies go to scope out the city, they are taken in by Rahab, a prostitute who protects them from those who seek to kill them.

Prostitution in the ancient world is not exactly like today. These weren't ladies standing on seedy street corners. Rather, they worked in the temples of pagan gods. It was believed that if you slept with the temple prostitute, it would entice the gods to cause the crops to grow. Not exactly what you learned in earth science club, I suppose. Suffice it to say, Rahab was an awfully sinful woman according to God's Law. She made a living by committing adultery as a form of idolatry.

But she had heard about the saving work of the God of Israel. She had heard and believed that He had conquered the Egyptians and rescued the Israelites. Such news had born in her a healthy, *faithful* fear of God so that when she encountered the people of this saving God, she was ready to help and support them in their time of need. She believed in God and her faith prompted her to act for the sake of God's people. Rahab's was a lively faith!

Let us not, however, miss the amazing grace of God in this story. Look at who it is that James holds up as the model of active faith: a pagan temple prostitute! God had mercy on her, He forgave her, and He used her to accomplish His purposes for His people. She was graciously included in God's work!

As we close this section on the relationship between faith and works, let us be encouraged by the example of Rahab. She was a poor sinner saved by a gracious God. Knowing God's gracious power drove her to work. So it is with us. A living faith comes, not from mustering up the energy to work harder, but by the work of the Holy Spirit who, through the Word, grants us Christ and all His benefits. It is from the gracious work of Christ for you—on the cross and in His Word and sacraments—that you are given a living faith.

Repent: Heavenly Father, forgive me for I am a poor sinner like Rahab. But like Rahab, I have received life and salvation from your gracious hand. Jesus has taken my impurities and washed them in His blood, making me clean and renewing my life. I pray that your daily forgiveness for my daily sins would empower me to daily walk in newness of life. AMEN.

Respond: After a heavy number of days in our study, today is an easy challenge. Just as Rahab opened the door for the Israelite spies, open the door for someone you don't know.

Receive: Just like Rahab the prostitute, you are a sinner, by nature and choice, whose lifestyle is not in line with God's Law. Yet it is God's will to use you for the sake of His kingdom. So like Rahab, His saving work has been proclaimed for you. Jesus conquered the enemies of His people on the cross and in His resurrection. It was carried out two thousand years ago. And it was carried out for you!

JUDGING TEACHERS

> *Not many of you should presume to be teachers, my brothers, because you know that we who teach will be judged more strictly.*

James 3:1

It is no small task to preach and teach the Word of God. Those who have received a call to do so find themselves under a holy scrutiny. It is the Lord who has called pastors to deliver a message for Him. Pastors are merely ambassadors of the heavenly embassy, proclaiming the message of their Lord (2 Cor. 5:20). Our Lord sends His ambassadors with a very specific message to proclaim: "The Christ will suffer and rise from the dead on the third day, and repentance and forgiveness of sins will be preached in his name to all nations, beginning at Jerusalem" (Luke 24:46–47). Repentance and forgiveness are for you because Jesus was crucified and raised. That is the message. That is the *only* message that pastors are to teach and preach.

Pretty simple, right? Not so fast. Pastors are sinners and are given to temptations just like everyone else. There are many things the devil sends to the preacher in order to get them to talk about anything but Christ from all of Scripture. Their own pet agendas creep in from time to time. Sometimes the sheep of God's flock desire to hear something beyond Christ. They want to have their itching ears scratched, as Paul warns Pastor Timothy (2 Tim. 4:3). So, they seek out pastors who will suit their own desires. In an effort to keep the flock, pastors may find themselves watering down the message. And frankly, our sinful hearts want to hear about something besides Jesus all the time. Pastors find it easier to discuss our idolatrous desires than to preach, again (!), that God is for us in Jesus Christ.

What we, pastors and parishioners alike, must be reminded of is that preaching and teaching the Word of God are not meant to help us get to know our pastor better nor to make us feel good about ourselves. It is most certainly not to make us merely happier with this idolatrous world. No, preaching is to deliver a message from God. Pastors are called to attack comfortable, obstinate sinners with God's Law to drive them to repentance and, then, to heal, restore, and forgive the broken, repentant sinners with God's Gospel. Paul instructs Timothy, "Preach the Word; be prepared in season and out of season; correct, rebuke and encourage—with great patience and careful instruction" (2 Tim. 4:2). On this basis, teachers and preachers of God's Word will be strictly judged. They will not be judged by how funny, engaging, or insightful they were. Rather, did they preach Christ crucified for sinners?

Repent: Gracious Father, forgive me for my itching ears. I confess that I have not hungered to hear your Word of grace because I have not taken my sin seriously enough. Have mercy on me, teach me to repent and believe the good news you have given to be proclaimed in your church. Raise up faithful pastors who boldly, faithfully, and stubbornly preach your Word alone. AMEN!

Respond: Commit yourself to pray for your pastor every day for one week. Find a day every week to pray for him, that he would faithfully deliver God's

Word to you and God's church. Pray, finally, for God to continue to raise up faithful pastors and for His dear church.

Receive: Jesus will not have His Word watered down. You should be damned for your sins. He's chosen instead to shed His blood for you. You are forgiven and beloved purely for His sake.

IT ONLY TAKES A SPARK

> *We all stumble in many ways. If anyone is never at fault in what he says, he is a perfect man, able to keep his whole body in check. When we put bits into the mouths of horses to make them obey us, we can turn the whole animal. Or take ships as an example. Although they are so large and are driven by strong winds, they are steered by a very small rudder wherever the pilot wants to go. Likewise the tongue is a small part of the body, but it makes great boasts. Consider what a great forest is set on fire by a small spark. The tongue also is a fire, a world of evil among the parts of the body. It corrupts the whole person, sets the whole course of his life on fire, and is itself set on fire by hell.*

James 3:2–6

It doesn't take much to start a forest fire. All you need is a small spark in the midst of some dry sticks and suddenly the whole area is aflame! Living in Southern California, I am familiar with how quickly a small spark can ignite a massive fire. One must be very careful when lighting matches in a field!

James says that a loose tongue, though small, is much like a firecracker in the woods—it can quickly start a fire and do a lot of damage. James is not just speaking of any old conversation, however. He is speaking of words that are spoken about God. False talk about God can cause big problems. As the church's history shows, small misunderstandings about God become big heresies that damage many lives. In the second commandment, we are told, "You shall not misuse the name of the Lord your God, for the Lord will not hold anyone guiltless who misuses His name" (Ex. 20:7). To speak where God has not spoken or to misrepresent God with our words will cause all kinds of problems, not only for our faith, but for the faith of others.

When we speak of God, we must speak of Him only where He has spoken. God speaks to us in the Word made flesh, Jesus Christ, whom the Spirit reveals to us in Scripture. To talk about God apart from Christ is to speak where God hasn't spoken. It is to take God's name in vain. But oh, what a joyful Word we have to speak! In Christ we speak of a God who loves, forgives, and saves. We speak of a God who sacrifices Himself for the sins committed against Him. We speak of love and reconciliation with God. Such words flow with refreshing waters that douse any destructive flame of false teaching. Why would we want to talk about anything else?

Repent: Gracious and almighty God, forgive me for my loose tongue. I have not spoken of you faithfully, and I have used your name for my own personal gain. Because your Son, Jesus Christ, spoke words of forgiveness from the cross for my sake, have mercy on me. Put your words in my mouth so that it will be filled with praise! AMEN.

Respond: Memorize a psalm or a hymn in an effort to train your tongue to sing God's praises.

Receive: God's truth is found in His Gospel: He is for you. His promise to you—you are forgiven—may sound small, but it is the power of God to heal the sick and raise the dead. This message may look weak and small to the world, but the announcement that declares you righteous falls from the same lips that spoke the creation into existence. God said, "Let there be light," and there was light. God said, "I forgive you for Christ's sake," and there, you, a sinner, were declared a saint.

WORDS MATTER

> *All kinds of animals, birds, reptiles and creatures*
> *of the sea are being tamed and have been tamed*
> *by man, but no man can tame the tongue. It is a*
> *restless evil, full of deadly poison.*

James 3:7–8

"Sticks and stones will break my bones, but words will never hurt me." Children will often employ this little rhyme in an effort to stave off mean-spirited words. Words can hurt. Insults and put downs have a way of getting into our heads and eating away at us. We wonder if they are true, if the insult is an accurate assessment of who we are. Even if it isn't true, we may ask, "What is wrong with me that someone would be driven to use such abusive language toward me?" Words can hurt.

We have tried to take away the impact of words in our culture by suggesting that words no longer mean anything. They are just sounds. As that consummate theologian Madonna once said, "Today is the last day that I am using words. They've gone out, lost their meaning, don't function anymore . . . Words are useless, especially sentences. They don't stand for anything. How could they explain how I feel?" Leaving beside the irony that Madonna's quote comes in the form of sentences, it is worth noting how we try to tear down the importance of words. Why would that be?

Perhaps it is because, despite what playground rhymes say, words can hurt. So often they are spit out of a poisonous tongue and cause us great harm. So, in an effort to ease the pain of such deadly poison, we just pretend like those words meant nothing. We try to make words meaningless. But we know deep down that it isn't true. Words do matter. Hurtful words do make a negative impact on us, just as loving words have a positive impact. James would have us be very careful in how we speak about God and to each other. He knows the damage words can cause.

Let us keep in mind that there is good reason to emphasize the importance of words. God Himself is a God who deals with us by means of words, even the Word made flesh. He is a speaking God who created the world by speaking it into existence: "God *said*, 'Let there be light'" (Gen. 1:3). This same speaking God who created the world by His Word has also created faith in your heart by the same forgiving Word. "For God, who said, 'Let light shine out of darkness,' made his light shine in our hearts to give us the light of the knowledge of the glory of God in the face of Christ" (2 Cor. 4:6). When the pastor baptized you and said, "I baptize you in the name of the Father, the Son, and the Holy Spirit," those were not empty words but promises from God Himself. His baptismal promise matters. His Word, which declares you righteous on account of Christ, matters so that, no matter what anyone else says, God's Word to you in Christ stands forever. His Word matters. It is a promise!

Repent: Forgive me, dear Father, for my words are not shaped by your Word of promise in Jesus Christ. I have hurt others by what I have said to them or about them. Forgive me for the sake of Jesus who used His words from the cross to say, "Father, forgive them, they know not what they do." Have mercy on me and teach me to use my words to your glory and for the benefit of my neighbors. AMEN.

Respond: Go a whole day without saying something negative about anyone.

Receive: Hear the Word of God: you are baptized. This means that no one else can define you, no accusation from Satan can condemn you, and no self-debasing shame has the final verdict over you. The final verdict over you was arrived at on Calvary, and in your baptism, the announcement was given: you are righteous for Christ's sake. You are baptized, and no one can say anything about it!

SALTY TONGUES

> *With the tongue we praise our Lord and Father, and with it we curse men, who have been made in God's likeness. Out of the same mouth come praise and cursing. My brothers, this should not be. Can both fresh water and salt water flow from the same spring? My brothers, can a fig tree bear olives, or a grapevine bear figs? Neither can a salt spring produce fresh water.*

James 3:9–12

Hypocrisy is one of the major criticisms leveled against Christians by those outside of the church. What's worse is there may be a great deal of truth behind that criticism. A hypocrite is a person who claims to have some great belief or virtue but then lives in such a way that is out of sync with the claimed belief. The old saying puts it this way: hypocrites talk the talk but don't walk the walk. There are many Christians in our world who are just this way.

Today, James warns us against such hypocrisy. The mouth that is found singing God's praises in the worship service should not be the same mouth that is gossiping about a brother or sister in the fellowship hall. The mouth that praises God for His beautiful creation should not be the mouth insulting God's creatures. The mouth that cries out for forgiveness should not be the mouth cursing fellow sinners. Fresh water and salt water cannot flow from the same stream.

Rather, those who are baptized with the fresh water of the Gospel should find words we use in worship (the liturgy) should be shaping the way we talk. If we believe the confession of sins to be true, then no one will be able to claim we are hypocrites. Why? Because when they see us sin, we can freely confess that it is because we are sinners, probably worse than they are. We can say that confidently because we know what our God does with sinners: He forgives them in the absolution. When we hear that our God forgives us for the sake of Christ, it shapes the way we speak to those who sin against us. The liturgy is formative. As beggars fed with the body and blood of Christ, we are led to give of ourselves to others. The words we hear and pray in worship are like a fountain of fresh water that is continuously poured into our hearts, which overflows into the way we speak and act toward others.

Repent: Heavenly Father, again I find myself confessing my sins to you. Though my confession demonstrates my sinful weakness, my life is a poor effort to prove how strong I am. I live to exalt my own righteousness and I am not humble in word or deed before my neighbors. Forgive me. May your Word of grace in Jesus shape the way I live and speak. AMEN.

Respond: Go out of your way to compliment three people today.

Receive: God speaks Words of mercy. Like the prophet Isaiah, you are a person with unclean lips (Isa. 6:1–6). But our God has had mercy on you, and when you eat the body and drink the blood of Christ with your mouth at the Lord's Supper, your lips are made pure. God uses His Word made flesh, Jesus Christ, to declare to you: you are forgiven!

THE WAY OF THE WISE

> *Who is wise and understanding among you? Let him show it by his good life, by deeds done in the humility that comes from wisdom.*

James 3:13

One Sunday, a pastor encouraged the congregation to invite people to join them at church next Sunday. Two members went out that week, intent on bringing their neighbors to church.

The first went out with his friend and boasted about how wonderful the church was. He boasted about how everyone got along, and no one ever fought. He talked about how every sermon was life-changing and the pastor was practically flawless. He waxed on about all the programs and events they had taking place and how everyone involved really had gotten their lives put together. He even began to talk about how a lot of his problems had gone away. His life had become wonderful because of this church. He told his friend that he should come next week.

Unfortunately, for some reason, the friend was not convinced and didn't attend.

The other person went out and invited her friend over for coffee. She asked her friend about her thoughts on church and why she didn't attend. She listened intently and didn't attempt to correct or change anything her friend said. She asked her about her thoughts on Jesus and, again, simply listened. Then, after pouring more coffee, she asked her friend if she would be interested in coming to her church, where they were going to be talking more about Jesus on Sunday. They could ride together and sit together. Afterward, she would take her friend out for lunch to discuss further what went on at church.

The friend wasn't sure but was certainly interested. The church member said she would call her on Saturday for an answer.

Both church members had great zeal for their neighbors, their church, and their Lord. But whose deeds came with humility and wisdom?

Repent: Heavenly Father, forgive me for being quick to act and slow to think. Give me a heart for those who do not know you and give me wisdom to speak faithfully with them about you. Grant this for the sake of your Son, Jesus Christ, my Lord. AMEN!

Respond: Have coffee with someone who doesn't attend church or doesn't believe and ask them about their thoughts on God, Jesus, and the church. Simply listen.

Receive: God is patient for your sake. He brings you to repentance so that your heart is made humble and your ears are opened to hear His wonderful news: Jesus Christ died for you. It may take a long time to get used to this reality. You will struggle the whole way. But Christ won't stop loving you and preaching His forgiveness into your ears. He who started this good work in you will bring it to completion.

SELFISH AMBITION

> *But if you harbor bitter envy and selfish ambition in your hearts, do not boast about it or deny the truth. Such "wisdom" does not come down from heaven but is earthly, unspiritual, of the devil.*

James 3:14–15

When Jesus walked among us, He did so fixated on the glory that was set before Him (Phil. 2:5–11). Resolutely, He set His course toward the cross, knowing that it was the place where He would shamefully suffer the wrath of God in the place of sinners so that sinners would receive His righteousness. Jesus came humbly and selflessly. He did not seek glory or fame. He sought sinners, all to the glory of God. God's glory saved sinners; this is what mattered to Jesus. That is why He came from heaven.

To lose everything and suffer great loss for the sake of others seems foolish to us, especially if the others are our enemies. Yet "when we were God's enemies, we were reconciled to him through the death of his Son" (Rom. 5:10). God's glorious Son set aside His glory and chose shame and a cross to save His enemies. That is the wisdom from above. That is love.

The world does not seek to glorify God or love the enemy. Rather, we have an entirely different motivation for living in our world—selfish ambition. As the iconic rock band Queen once sang, "I want it all! And I want it now!" We want to be on top of everyone else. If in the process of realizing our selfish goals someone else hinders our efforts, we grow angry, even bitter. Hatred wells up inside of us, and we seek to harm the other person, just as they have harmed us.

Such bitterness and selfishness are wicked, James says. It is earthly—that is, concerned only with this world—having no regard for eternity. It is unspiritual—that is, not produced by the Holy Spirit but our own selfish hearts (Matt. 15:19). It is of the devil—that is, carried out with no concern for God, much to the devil's delight. Add it all up and this equals sinful foolishness.

The wisdom of the world entreats us to live for today, care only for yourself, get the biggest toys, have the most money, and so on. It is utterly selfish. It is utterly foolish. Christ is our wisdom. Christ suffers for the sake of His enemies. He loves them so that they might be saved. True wisdom is found in Jesus who loves at all costs. Even to the point of dying on a cross in a way that is utterly foolish to this earthly, unspiritual, devilish world.

Repent: Father of all mercy and grace, hear my pleas for the sake of your Son, Jesus Christ, who loved me and gave Himself up for me. I have lived in rebellion and sin. At one time, I was your enemy. But through the blood of Christ, we have been reconciled so I can, by your grace, call you Father! Teach me, oh, Father, to so love my enemies. I pray for those who persecute me and anger me. Help me love them and remove all bitterness from my heart. I ask this in Jesus' most precious name. AMEN.

Respond: Every day for the next week pray for a person who you don't like. Ask the Lord to teach you how to love them and to forgive them if necessary, even though you don't think they deserve it.

Receive: Jesus Christ is the wisdom of God. Though it may look like foolishness to the world, God has chosen to save the weakest and most foolish of sinners by means of a weak, humiliating cross. God was pleased to be found suffering in Christ for the salvation of a rebellious, thankless people. God was foolish enough, if you can believe it, to do this for you!

SELFISH AMBITION VERSUS HUMBLE LOVE

> *For where you have envy and selfish ambition, there you find disorder and every evil practice. But the wisdom that comes from heaven is first of all pure; then peace-loving, considerate, submissive, full of mercy and good fruit, impartial and sincere.*

James 3:16–17

I once had a conversation with someone who worked in Washington, DC. She said it was a very depressing place to work. Wide-eyed young adults looking to change the nation naively come to the capital ready to act on their ideals. She said that within a year, they have learned that if you want someone to scratch your back, you must scratch theirs, even if that means compromising your ideals. Make no mistake: it almost always means compromising your ideals. Ideals become selfish ambitions, and suddenly the only thing that matters is winning, no matter who you hurt in the process. It becomes a game of kill or be killed.

Such wisdom does not come from heaven. Life in the kingdom of God is not one of willpower and selfish ambition. Here, the mentality is not kill or be killed but sacrificially die for the sake of loving your neighbor! After all, that is what our Lord and God has done for us! Christ did not become our Lord by exerting His power and authority over us. But Jesus, "being found in appearance as a man, he humbled himself and became obedient to death—even death on a cross! Therefore, God exalted him to the highest place and gave him the name that is above every name" (Phil. 2:8–9). Christ's glory is found, not in His exertion of power (which is rightfully His) over His creatures but in dying in the place of sinners.

With the sacrificial Lamb serving as our Lord, life in the kingdom is radically different from that of the world. Wisdom here does not say that we should win at all costs. Wisdom here says that we should love at all costs. Pure, heavenly wisdom grants us lives that are "peace-loving, considerate, submissive, full of mercy and good fruit, impartial and sincere." Such lives may not get a bill passed in Washington, but they certainly glorify our Father in heaven and bless those around us. Just ask Jesus!

Repent: God of all grace, forgive me for my pride and selfish ambition. I have not reflected the humility of your Son in the way I treat my neighbors; rather, I have used them for selfish gain. Teach me to lead a life of humility and service. I pray this in the name of your Son, Jesus Christ, who humbly died in my place. AMEN.

Respond: Next time you must stand in line, let two people behind you cut in front of you.

Receive: God's Word is powerful. With it, He has created universes, He has stilled the sea, and He has judged kingdoms. His Word always accomplishes what it says. What wonderful news it is to know that with this Word, so full of terrifying power, God chooses to say, "I forgive you for the sake of Jesus Christ."

MAKING PEACE

> *Peacemakers who sow in peace raise a harvest of righteousness.*
>
> **James 3:18**

Jesus comes as a peacemaker. Peacemakers do their work between two parties at war. We are born at enmity with God. King David once said it this way: "Surely I was sinful at birth, sinful from the time my mother conceived me" (Ps. 51:5). We are born as His enemies, dead in our sins and trespasses (Eph. 2:1–3). Apart from Christ, we live in constant anarchy against our divine Lord and Creator. We always talk about humanity's "fall" into sin like we tripped over a branch and just "fell" into a hole we call sin. But as theologian Gerhard Forde says, that fall was upward. It was no accident but a treasonous act of rebellion against God. We sought to overthrow the throne of heaven. We are at war with God by nature and choice.

Such rebellious action places us under God's wrath. In this war, God will win. We have the weaker, smaller army. He is God. He is like the unstoppable army of Alexander the Great. We are like a box of arrogant toy soldiers. All hope is lost for the rebels.

But in an unbelievable act of mercy, the offended God makes peace. The Lord of hosts (i.e., of the angelic armies) makes an offering of peace: Himself! He is the offering of reconciliation who creates peace! "God was reconciling the world to himself in Christ, not counting men's sins against them" (2 Cor. 5:19). This work of peacemaking has raised a harvest of righteousness. In other words, in offering His life as a sacrificial peace offering and dying in our place, Jesus has also given us the gift of His righteousness. So that, through the death of Christ, God sees us as saints clothed in the righteousness of Christ and not as treasonous sinners.

We have been reconciled to God through the blood of Christ, our peacemaker. And now, Paul says, "He has committed to us the message of reconciliation" (2 Cor. 5:19). We go as those clothed in the righteousness of Christ, at peace with God, and proclaim His peace to those still at war. The God they fight against has forgiven them for Christ's sake! Let us be the ones to proclaim this peace to them!

Repent: Heavenly Father, what gracious work your Son has done so that I no longer need to fear you but can call you my Father. Forgive me for my rebellious sins and use me to bring peace with your Word, just as it has been brought to me. I thank you for your grace to sinners like me. AMEN!

Respond: Commit to praying for the members of the armed forces who seek to keep peace for our country.

Receive: The Lord Jesus has made peace between you and God. Because of Christ's shed blood for you, you are no longer an enemy but a child of the Heavenly Father. Jesus has reconciled you by taking your sin away from you and God's wrath away from you. God has no wrath left for you. You are at peace with God through Jesus!

ASKING

> *What causes fights and quarrels among you?*
> *Don't they come from your desires that battle*
> *within you? You want something but don't get it.*
> *You kill and covet, but you cannot have what you*
> *want. You quarrel and fight. You do not have,*
> *because you do not ask God. When you ask,*
> *you do not receive, because you ask with wrong*
> *motives, that you may spend what you get on*
> *your pleasures.*

James 4:1–3

Here, at the beginning of chapter 4, we see that the love of worldly pleasure is giving cause to sin. James is speaking to a specific situation where greed and base desires had led to fighting (and even murder!) in the church. However, what he says is very true in our own world. We live in a pleasure-driven world. We are told that we can have all the lustful, covetous desires we could ever dream of . . . if. *If* you just have enough money, *if* you just have enough power, *if* you just have enough success, then all your wildest dreams will come true! Sure, we hear the stories about the devastating fall the rich and famous have endured, but that won't change our goals. We will be able to handle our fame and wealth. We will be able to indulge the desires of our heart if we could just get a little more money, success, and so on.

But "if" never seems to come. At least, it doesn't come easy, so we grow frustrated and angry. We find shortcuts to the "if" life. Shortcuts that may not be morally sound but that do put us on the fast track to success. We hurt our neighbor, undercut our coworker, spread rumors, and so on to get what we want. A little lie never hurt anyone (or it will only hurt someone a little bit), but it certainly will help me achieve my goals!

All this selfishness flows from a heart of sin. This is a life that lacks faith because it acts as if true happiness is both defined by the world and dependent on my success. Such an attitude comes from a heart that does not believe that God is a good Father who gives good gifts. The problem is that we don't want just our daily bread from God, we want power, success, and (more) money. Our goals are defined by the world; our lives are defined by our goals and not by God's gifts!

But God gives more grace and beckons us to call on Him for our daily bread and needs in this life. Our God is a good Father who hears our prayers and answers them in love and wisdom. He does not hear the prayer for selfish, worldly greed because such a prayer is sinful. You see, God is better and more gracious than that. He won't cater to our sins. Rather, Jesus says, "Which of you, if his son asks for bread will give him a stone? Or if he asks for a fish, will give him a snake? If you, though you are evil, know how to give good gifts to your children, how much more will your Father in heaven give good gifts to those who ask Him?" (Matt. 7:9–11). This is true even of forgiveness! There is forgiveness for you, even when you let the world set the agenda and don't look to God our Father, who has given us the greatest gift of all, Jesus Christ crucified, to provide our daily bread.

Repent: Heavenly Father, I confess to you the sinful desires of my heart. I confess that I don't trust you as I ought. I confess that I believe true contentment is found in power and success. Forgive such selfish desires. I praise you for Jesus who set aside power and glory and chose a cross to forgive my selfish desires. For Christ's sake, I pray that you would teach me true contentment and joy in your Son Jesus. AMEN.

Respond: Do a random act of kindness in secret. For example, bring in your neighbor's trash cans, anonymously leave Starbucks on your coworker's desk, pay for the person behind you at the drive-thru, and so on.

Receive: Jesus has reconciled you to the Father. God looks on you as His dear, beloved child. Jesus stands to intercede and pray for your forgiveness. What's more, He's given you access to the Father's ear so that God will hear your prayers and answer for your good. When you ask for food, He provides. When you ask for forgiveness, He replies, "Dear child, you are forgiven for Christ's sake."

ADULTEROUS PEOPLE

> *You adulterous people, don't you know that*
> *friendship with the world is hatred toward God?*
> *Anyone who chooses to be a friend of the world*
> *becomes an enemy of God. Or do you think*
> *Scripture says without reason that the spirit he*
> *caused to live in us envies intensely?*

James 4:4–5

Adulterous people? Geez, James, ease up! Why the strong language? James is quite wise in use of such harsh language today. He's picking up on a common Old Testament theme where "adultery" is used to describe idolatry (read Hos. 1–3). God loved Israel like a husband loves his wife. He rescued her, protected her, provided for her, and cared for with tender mercy. Israel responded by worshipping false gods, breaking God's commandments, and indulging their sinful desires with the very gifts God had provided for them. (Incidentally, adultery was a very appropriate analogy as worship of false gods consisted of fornication in the temples that belonged to those "gods.") God loved Israel with all His heart, and she abused that love, seeking other suitors who treated her shamefully. God was thus righteously jealous for Israel. He loved her, wanted to provide for her and give her all good things. But she sought pleasure in the world. As a result of her faithlessness, Israel was cast off and sent into exile.

The people of God never learn. In the New Testament, the church as the new Israel is called the bride of Christ (Eph. 5:21–33; Rev. 19:7, 21:2, 9). Yet like our ancestors in the faith, we find ourselves seeking "friendship" with the world. Do not think that James is saying here that we should not enjoy the goodness of God's creation. We are certainly to enjoy what God has made and rejoice in it. However, we are not to worship it.

The creation is not supposed to replace God. When the gifts of God begin to replace God, they become idols: the need for money becomes greed, sex becomes pornography, rest becomes laziness, and gifts become trash. In our sin, we turn the gifts that God gives—which are supposed to result in worship— into gods themselves, something to distract us from God. We do so because we love the immediate gratification they provide more than the grace of God! In this way, we are like a woman who marries a man in order to use him for his money and not because she loves him.

Such a life will produce sorrow, frustration, and bitterness. Our idolatrous/ adulterous eyes wander away from our Heavenly Bridegroom who loves us and has given all things for us. As Paul says of Jesus when instructing hus-bands, "Christ loved the church and gave himself up for her to make her holy, cleansing her by the washing with water through the word and to present her to himself as a radiant church, without stain or wrinkle or any other blemish, but holy and blameless" (Eph. 5:25–27). We are a sinful, adulterous bride. But we have a Bridegroom who has washed us clean of our stains by giving Himself up for us. His love is all we need. In this love, we lack nothing!

Repent: Dear Jesus, for the sake of your holy, innocent, and bitter sufferings, have mercy on me. I confess to you that I have wandered from your love in thought, word, and deed. Forgive me, again, and teach me to cling to you in faith, to trust your love, and to realize that you are all that I need. AMEN.

Respond: Read Hosea 1–3 and memorize 2:19–20. Rejoice that this is what Jesus has done for you on the cross and in your baptism!

Receive: The Lord Jesus is faithful to His promises. When He baptized you, He promised to present you as holy and blameless to God. He stands on that promise, and you live in that promise. You are holy and blameless, forgiven and made clean because He has washed you in His blood and united Himself to you with His promises.

CLEAN HANDS AND A PURE HEART

> *But he gives us more grace. That is why Scripture says: "God opposes the proud but gives grace to the humble." Submit yourselves, then, to God. Resist the devil, and he will flee from you. Come near to God and he will come near to you. Wash your hands, you sinners, and purify your hearts, you double-minded.*
>
> **James 4:6–8**

The last two days, we have heard James show us the dangers of falling in love with the world. Today, with one simple phrase, James proclaims how God is greater than all the empty promises that the world spits at us: "But He gives us more grace." The world gives more demands, more expectations, and more empty promises. God makes promises full of grace and mercy. The gifts the world gives never satisfy. Worldly pursuits always leave us wanting and desiring more. God graciously gives us all we need in Jesus Christ!

The world and the devil are working together in this. The devil will promise you the world! But he is a liar and cannot give what he promises. He tells you he has your best interests in mind, but really, he hates you and wants you dead. So, the devil will never let you arrive anywhere, he will never let you find satisfaction. (It is no small irony that the same Rolling Stones who sang "I Can't Get No Satisfaction" also sang "Sympathy for the Devil.") Satan will always tell you that you could have more, do more, and be more than you already are. He says, "You are worthless. You aren't living life to the fullest. You aren't even doing enough for God. How could He love you if you can't love Him enough?" The devil is our accuser who is always looking for our destruction. He is always trying to distract us from the sufficiency of Christ, who gives more grace!

But Christ has silenced the devil. When John wrote his book of Revelation and was describing the victory of Christ's cross, he said this of the devil: "Then I heard a loud voice in heaven say: 'Now have come the salvation and the power and the kingdom of our God, and the authority of his Christ. For the accuser of our brothers, who accuses them before our God day and night, has been hurled down'" (Rev. 12:10). Satan has been defeated by the blood of Christ. His accusations against you have been silenced, as Christ's death paid for your sins and has removed your guilt. The death of Jesus is sufficient. He gives more grace.

Repent: Heavenly Father, I confess that I oftentimes feel as though Christ is not enough for me. I fear that I have sinned too much to be saved. I fear that I haven't done enough to get to heaven. I believe the lies of the devil that would distract me from your promises that tell me Jesus has taken away all my sins and His righteousness has been granted to me as a gift. Forgive my doubt and grant me faithful trust! AMEN.

Respond: Throughout this series, you may have begun to feel guilty that you have not completed all the challenges. You may have even worried that you weren't a very good Christian because of your lack of effort. Your sufficiency is in Christ! Whatever challenges you have not yet fulfilled are canceled for you. Today's challenge is to forget the challenges you have not yet completed.

Receive: You are in Christ. This means God will not entertain any accusation the devil hurls toward you. Those sins you feel especially guilty for, those ones that terrify your conscience and keep you up at night? Jesus died for those. He forgives you. And He is not bringing them up anymore. Your conscience has been washed in the blood of Jesus. Satan's accusations are silenced for you. You are free.

HUMBLE YOURSELVES

> *Grieve, mourn and wail. Change your laughter to mourning and your joy to gloom. Humble yourselves before the Lord, and he will lift you up.*

James 4:9–10

In his epistle, James has demonstrated to us why we need to repent: our sin! Sometimes, however, the true meaning of repentance is lost on us. We view repentance as nothing more than a password that gets us out of trouble with God. But repentance is not merely saying the right words with our mouths, as if God could be fooled by a false confession. Rather, repentance is the faithful response to the preaching of God's Law. To put it another way, repentance is what happens when we believe what God says about us is true: we are sinners. Repentance isn't something we kind of conjure up inside of ourselves. We don't just try to make ourselves feel bad. No, repentance is what happens when we hear about God's anger toward sin and, worse, His wrath toward faithless sinners!

The preaching of the Law—that is, God's will for how His creatures should live—is like being told by your doctor that you have cancer. You know your body should be healthy, but it isn't. Such news produces fear and response.

"What can I do? What's next?" Thank God we live in a day and age where there are many treatments for cancer and the doctor will typically have a plan to move forward. Things aren't so hopeful when it comes to the Law of God. Under the proclamation of the Law, we have no hope, no path forward. The Law kills us. It leaves us dead. The Law tells us that God loves the righteous and hates the wicked. The wicked will suffer His wrath (Ps. 11:1–7). The Law diagnoses us with wickedness and leaves us for dead. Such news causes grief, mourning, and wailing. Laughter turns to mourning and joy to gloom. It causes us to despair of all righteousness inside of ourselves. We are humbled. We are killed. Not even our repentance can save us now! But God is not finished talking.

By itself, the Law that leaves us without hope is not the last Word. Christ is! When we find ourselves in despair under God's Law, we cry out for mercy, and God responds by being born of a virgin. In fact, it was Mary who sang, "He has brought down rulers from their thrones but has *lifted up the humble*" (Luke 1:52). Jesus comes to fulfill what the Law demands of us: both its commands and its consequences. He lives it out perfectly and yet dies under its condemnations. This death we sinners deserved. "He was born of a woman, born under law, to redeem those under law" (Gal. 4:4–5). The Law kills us and leaves us with no hope, nowhere to turn. But God turns toward us in Christ Jesus and removes the condemnation of the Law, giving us new life! He turns away from sin (repents!) in our place. All that God demands of us in the Law is given to us in Christ! He lifts us up!

Repent: I repent, dear God, for all my sins with which I have offended you! I deserve your wrath and condemnation. I hear your will and I am brought low and made humble. Forgive me for the sake of your Son, Jesus, who was made low to the point of death on the cross. I thank you that His blood was shed for me. I pray that your Law and Gospel daily fill my ears, so I have a life of repentance and rejoicing. AMEN!

Respond: Continue looking through the Ten Commandments in the Small Catechism. Write down whatever sins are weighing heavy on you and bring it to church on Sunday. When the pastor proclaims the absolution, rip the paper to shreds.

Receive: The Lord Jesus has called you to repent. Your repentance, however, is never perfect enough to merit His forgiveness. So, He turned away from all sin and temptation for you. What is more, He has now given you credit for His faithfulness! You are forgiven, even for your flimsy repentance!

JUDGMENTALISM

> *Brothers, do not slander one another. Anyone who speaks against his brother or judges him speaks against the law and judges it. When you judge the law, you are not keeping it, but sitting in judgment on it. There is only one Lawgiver and Judge, the one who is able to save and destroy. But you—who are you to judge your neighbor?*

James 4:11–12

Television is making judges of us all. This struck me as I was watching *American Idol* a number of years ago. I smugly analyzed and spoke my verdict over each singer—as the show was designed to let me do. But then, after Steven Tyler said something that made no grammatical sense, Jennifer Lopez began to praise a singer that I thought was awful. I said, "What is she thinking? That was terrible!" Suddenly, I was judging the judges! When Randy—in my judgment—rightly said that it wasn't his favorite of the night, the audience booed. "Why do they always do that?" I thought. "They don't know anything!" Another judgment! The worst part? I have no credentials that would qualify me to vote with any semblance of expertise. All I have is my opinion. But since

I have a remote and two ears, I cast judgment in my living room like I am a record producer!

Judgmentalism is an epidemic in our society. We judge everything. We even judge our brothers and sisters in the church. We look down on them and gossip about them. Sometimes, in our self-righteous benevolence, we give "godly" advice on how this person can improve themselves to become a better Christian . . . well, a better Christian by our judgment anyway. In our worst moments, we'll find ourselves thinking, "Why are they here? Are they even a Christian? If so, they certainly aren't as mature or sanctified as I am!"

We spend a lot of time trying to ignore the planks in our eyes so we can condescendingly stare at the specks in the eyes of others (Matt. 7:3–5). Judgment may be funny when watching *American Idol*, but it is deadly in the church. It causes despair among those who worry about their faith and pride among those who think they have this whole Christian life figured out. To be sure, we are to lovingly correct one another when we fall into sin. But it is not ours to judge the faith of our brothers and sisters. That belongs to God! He is the one who is able to save and destroy.

When we find ourselves being judgmental toward our brothers and sisters, we find ourselves opposed to God. His judgment toward sinners took place on the cross. The guilty verdict against sinners was declared on Jesus as He was condemned in your place and in the place of all your brothers and sisters in the church. God has cast His judgment for all of us on Christ. And His verdict? You are holy for Christ's sake.

Repent: Heavenly Father, gracious Judge, you have had mercy on me for the sake of your Son Jesus who took my guilty verdict and died in my place. You have declared me—a sinner—to be righteous. Please forgive my constant judgmentalism. Teach me to let your judgment stand for my brothers and sisters. Help me love and not judge. AMEN.

Respond: Once again, go an entire day without saying something negative about anyone.

Receive: You are surrounded by people who judge and condemn. Sometimes their condemning eye falls on you. But fear not! For God sees you too. But He looks on you through the shed blood of Jesus Christ. He took God's judgment for you and away from you. Because He was judged guilty in your place; you stand innocent before God by grace alone!

WHAT ABOUT MY PLANS?

> *Now listen, you who say, "Today or tomorrow we will go to this or that city, spend a year there, carry on business and make money." Why, you do not even know what will happen tomorrow. What is your life? You are a mist that appears for a little while and then vanishes. Instead, you ought to say, "If it is the Lord's will, we will live and do this or that." As it is, you boast and brag. All such boasting is evil.*

James 4:13–15

For some of us, this may be the most terrifying passage in the Bible. We are scheduling freaks! Some of us have our next six months scheduled to the minute. We have calendars on the wall and day planners in the car, and the calendars on our phones are synced up to office and home computers. We schedule meetings, business trips, vacations, family time, and so on. Sports for the kids keep us on a demanding schedule. And we love it!

Why? I mean, it sounds so demanding to be so beholden to a schedule. However, it gives us a sense of control over our lives. The future, which is so uncertain and so unpredictable is suddenly in the palm of my hand (on my iPhone) and under my management. I am the master of my destiny!

But what happens if, God (!) forbid, our plans get changed? What if I lose my iPhone in the toilet? What if the airline we're flying for vacation goes out of business? What if tragedy strikes? What if I lose my job? What if the economy crashes and I can't retire like I had planned? What if someone dies or gets cancer? Our plans would be ruined. Our calendars would be exposed for the shams that they are. We cannot plan our future; we do not control our destiny.

"Instead," James says, "you ought to say, 'If it is the Lord's will, we will live and do this or that.'" This is not an easy thought for us. It is not comfortable to leave our lives in the hands of Someone so unpredictable, so unmanageable, and so holy. What if God doesn't do things the way I want Him to? What if our calendars don't sync? What if I lose control and things fall apart? Can I still trust Him in the midst of that?

This is an uneasy thought to be sure. But remember the God who holds your future is the God who has promised you eternity. This is the God who has loved you enough to send His Son to take your sins and prepare a place in the heavenly kingdom for you. His will is certainly unpredictable, unmanageable, and holy. In other words, it is gracious, whether we like it or not! God's grace just doesn't fit into our schedules! It is too good. Hear and believe that He who controls the future controls it graciously for you!

Repent: Heavenly Father, I confess that I work very hard to control my future. I have a hard time letting go of my plans and trusting you to care for me. Yet with the events of my life, I am daily reminded that you are in control, even when it seems like everything is out of control. Teach me to trust in your grace. Carry me through whatever comes my way in your grace, all the way to eternity! AMEN!

Respond: Plan a day where you make no plans (how ironic!). Don't be upset if things come up to ruin your planned unplanned day!

Receive: Before the foundations of the world, God chose to send Jesus Christ to die for you. He has had your salvation planned before your sinful heart took its first beat and your sinful lungs filled with breath. He has not only planned and accomplished your salvation in Jesus Christ; He has prepared a place for you in His presence for eternity.

LOVE THE LAW?

> *Anyone, then, who knows the good he ought to do and doesn't do it, sins.*

James 4:17

In this short verse, James gives a brief summary of the letter. The main argument of James' epistle is finished. Chapter 5 will address other matters James seeks to deal with. What he has been discussing up to this point—the idea that the life of faith produces good works—is summarized here.

One thing that has been made abundantly clear in this letter is that we who are declared to be saints through the blood of Jesus are still sinners. We will be 100 percent sinners and 100 percent saints until Christ comes again. God's Law always accuses us of our lack of righteousness. So, if we are sinners, even as Christians, how can we ever do the right thing? How can we do the good we ought to do if we are still sinners?

There is a tension in the Christian life that we must be aware of: We who are forgiven for our sins by God have also been born into a new life in Christ. At the same time, we who are baptized into the faith are also going to battle sin for the rest of our lives. We have been raised to a new life wherein we are enabled, by the Holy Spirit who is at work in us, to do the good God wants us to do. As we have said ad nauseam, such works don't produce salvation, but they do come from the Savior. The Law of God, which always accuses the sinner in us, also guides the saint in us. We can actually hear the Law of God and rejoice in its directing effects! As it says in Psalm 119:47, "I delight in your commands because I love them."

Knowing that God has graciously and fully saved us through the righteousness of Christ drives us to ask, "What do I do now?" Since salvation has been completely accomplished and God needs nothing from His creatures, God directs us with His Law in how we should serve and love our neighbors. His Law, which cannot save us, does direct us in acts of righteousness. It no longer condemns the saint in us so that we are free to do the good we ought to do. Will we find ourselves sinning? Of course. Read Romans 7 to get a good picture of what the Christian life will look like. But the reality of sin is hardly an excuse to cease from loving our neighbor. As Martin Luther said, "It is impossible for [faith] not to be doing good works incessantly. It does not ask whether good works are to be done, but before the question is asked, it has already done them."[3] Faith without works is dead, but you have been raised to a new life of living faith with Christ!

Repent: Almighty God, your Law is good and wise. I know the good that you have called me to do. But I confess that I do not find my hands doing the very things my heart knows are right. In this, I sin. I thank you that through your Son's death and resurrection, you have rescued me from this body of death. AMEN!

---

3. Martin Luther, *Luther's Works*, ed. Jaroslav Jan Pelikan, Hilton C. Oswald, and Helmut T. Lehmann, vol. 35, *Word and Sacrament I* (Philadelphia: Fortress, 1999), 370–71.

Respond: For the next week, pray that God will show you how to express His will toward someone you love. For example, pray that God will show you a different way to show love to someone in your family every day this week.

Receive: Jesus was tempted just like you in every way, just without sin. He always knew the right thing to do, and He did it perfectly. His life was lived perfectly in obedience to His Father. His Father willed for Jesus to die for you so that the sins you have committed, the wrong you have done, is washed away in Christ's blood. You are forgiven!

ROTTEN WEALTH

Now listen, you rich people, weep and wail because of the misery that is coming upon you. Your wealth has rotted, and moths have eaten your clothes. Your gold and silver are corroded. Their corrosion will testify against you and eat your flesh like fire. You have hoarded wealth in the last days. Look! The wages you failed to pay the workmen who mowed your fields are crying out against you. The cries of the harvesters have reached the ears of the Lord Almighty. You have lived on earth in luxury and self-indulgence. You have fattened yourselves in the day of slaughter. You have condemned and murdered innocent men, who were not opposing you.

James 5:1–6

It is not a sin to be rich. To be sure, wealth can be the cause of many problems. St. Paul tells Timothy, "People who want to get rich fall into temptation and a trap and into many foolish and harmful desires that plunge men into ruin and destruction. For the love of money is a root of all kinds of evil. Some people, eager for money, have wandered from the faith and pierced themselves with many griefs" (1 Tim. 6:9–10). So, though it is not a sin to have money, money can easily become a god to us, the worship of which causes us to wander from the faith.

Today in our reading, James is not talking to rich Christians. He is talking to those whose god is their belly (Phil. 3:19). They worship money. James is proclaiming in harsh and frightening terms the end result of such false worship: impending misery. Money and wealth are fleeting. The riches and the glories of this world are passing away and are doomed to destruction. Clinging to idols bound for destruction will lead idolaters to destruction. This is true not just for the faithless rich but for anyone who clings to any kind of a false god.

What is more, this group of people James is writing against is attacking the church of God! They have lived in luxury and self-indulgence at the cost of the lives of God's "workmen." They have condemned and murdered innocent men. Incidentally, a better translation of "innocent men" is "the Righteous Man." It is likely that James is associating their persecution of the church with the crucifixion of Jesus Himself (see also Matt. 25:45 and Acts 9:4)![4]

Thus, the sins that James is dealing with here are those that come from the love of wealth—namely, false worship and the persecution of Christ and His church! The church of God can expect persecution and suffering, just as her Lord endured. The world will hate the church just as it hated her Lord. But Jesus says, "Blessed are those who are persecuted because of righteousness, for theirs is the kingdom of heaven" (Matt. 5:10). True wealth and riches are for us found in Christ. But let us not miss James' harsh condemnations today.

---

4. "It seems best to take this as a reference to Jesus primarily and to persecuted Christians secondarily. James' Christology involves the church suffering at the hands of God's enemies." David P. Scaer, *James the Apostle of Faith: A Primary Christological Epistle for the Persecuted Church* (St. Louis: Concordia, 1983), 122–23.

God will deal justly with those who have rejected His grace and persecuted His family for the sake of wealth.

Repent: Heavenly Father, I thank you that you have rescued me from darkness and brought me into the kingdom of the Son you love. I confess to you that I am often tempted by the luxuries of this world. Forgive me for being drawn to such false worship and teach me to rejoice in the merciful gift of your dear Son Jesus, my Lord. AMEN!

Respond: Next time you are out, leave a very large tip.

Receive: The Lord has used all the wealth of heaven to purchase you from sin and death. He did not use gold nor silver but His own precious blood. You belong to Him and nothing in this world, especially no persecutors, will be able to separate you from the love of God that is yours in Christ Jesus!

THE WAITING

> *Be patient, then, brothers, until the Lord's coming. See how the farmer waits for the land to yield its valuable crop and how patient he is for the autumn and spring rains. You too, be patient and stand firm, because the Lord's coming is near.*
>
> **James 5:7–8**

Perhaps the hardest day of the year for children is December 18. Why? It is one week before Christmas! You are so close to the most exciting day of the year! But oh, that next week seems like it will take an eternity! Or how about the last day of work before you go on vacation? It takes forever for 5:00 p.m. to come around, doesn't it? As Tom Petty once sang, "The waiting is the hardest part!"

Often, this is the feeling in the church when it comes to the return of Christ. We look at the world around us falling apart, we grow older and our bodies begin to fall apart, our struggle with sin just won't seem to go away, and we may find ourselves looking at the clock and crying out, "How long, oh, Lord?" Think of how much the anticipation must have been felt by the church James is addressing. They had fled their homes to avoid persecution for their faith. They were never sure if they would live through another day or be killed for confessing Jesus as their Lord. They had no security and no home. One wonders if we can comprehend the depths of their desire to be at home with the Lord.

In the midst of struggle and trial, it becomes easy for us to grow frustrated and anxious toward God. We may even begin to question His love! When things are really rough and it seems as if we are in the pit of hell, we find ourselves crying out with the psalmist, "How long, O Lord? Will you forget me forever? How long will you hide your face from me?" (Ps. 13:1).

God's gracious answer to the "how long" question is found in the mouth of Jesus: "In my Father's house are many rooms; if it were not so, I would have told you. I am going there to prepare a place for you. And if I go and prepare a place for you, I will come back and take you to be with me that you also may be where I am" (John 14:2–3). We don't know how long the Lord will allow our world to continue to run like it is, but no matter what may come, we can persevere knowing that our dear Lord Jesus, who suffered on the cross, also rose again on the third day. In doing so, He prepared a place for us in eternity. We can cling to this promise because we know that Christ is clinging to us with His nail-pierced hand. No matter how long we must wait, we know that Christ is holding us the whole time.

Repent: Heavenly Father, I confess to you my impatience. In my weariness with the strains and trials of this life, I find myself doubting your promises and giving in to sin. Forgive me for not trusting you through my trials. I thank you that Jesus endured the cross for me, taking my sin and my shame. I pray that your Holy Spirit would empower me to endure my trials and I praise you that you will never let me go. AMEN!

Respond: Shut off the TV tonight and talk to someone for one hour.

Receive: "The Lord is not slow to fulfill his promise as some count slowness, but is patient toward you, not wishing that any should perish, but that all should reach repentance" (2 Peter 3:9). The Lord is patient toward you and, on your confession of sins, is not slow to have the good news proclaimed to you: Jesus has already died and risen for your salvation! You are forgiven now for His sake!

THE JUDGE

> *Don't grumble against each other, brothers, or you will be judged. The Judge is standing at the door!*

James 5:9

Once again, today James takes up the topic of judgment. If there is one thing we fear, it is judgment. We get very defensive when we are judged by others. Consider how you feel when you go in for a job interview. Typically, if we really want the job, we go in with some level of nervousness because we are about to be judged. So, we dress ourselves up very nicely, we put on our best behavior, and we present a resume that makes us look like we will be of great benefit to this would-be employer. All this is done in an effort to be judged worthy of getting the job. There is just one thing we can't control: the one carrying out the interview. We cannot control the judge. That is why we fear judgment; it is beyond our control. We can dress ourselves up as nicely as we'd like, but we cannot control the judge!

If this is how we feel going into a job interview, how much more nerve-racking is it to stand before the Judge of the universe? The Second Coming of Jesus is immanent and has been so for roughly two thousand years. We confess every Sunday that when He returns, He will judge both the living and the dead. This is a very intimidating prospect for us because God knows our hearts, He knows our thoughts, and He knows our deeds. All that stuff we thought was hidden and that we've gotten away with is known to Him. Even when we attempt to cover our sin and shame before God by dressing ourselves with good works and religious activity, we cannot tip the scales in our favor. Trying to use our good works to cover our sin is like a man with ten DUIs on his record wearing a suit to an interview for school bus drivers. The suit is a weak attempt to cover the guilt.

The judgment seat of Christ could be a terrifying place for sinners, not just because of our guilt, but especially because we cannot control the Judge! It is His decision whether we are declared guilty or innocent. He has given us the standard in the Law we are to follow, and we know we've failed. So, no matter how much we dress ourselves up, we cannot control the Judge's decision.

We cannot control what God knows about us. We cannot control His judgment of us. We simply receive the verdict: "not guilty." Wait . . . *not guilty?* The verdict is declared by a gracious Judge who forgives sinners for the sake of Christ's death on the cross. We could never cover our sins, so Christ covers them in His blood! We could never dress ourselves up enough to hide our shame, so Christ clothes us in His righteousness! We cannot control how the Judge will reach His verdict, but the Judge who is in control forgives! As we await the immanent return of Christ, we do so in great anticipation, knowing that God's verdict has been declared on the cross. We have been judged forgiven.

Repent: Father, forgive me for my lack of faith in your grace. Forgive me for trying to cover up my sins instead of confessing them. Forgive me for trying to control my fate instead of trusting your Son who has promised to save me. Teach me to trust in you and to look forward to your Son's return with confidence. Help me forgive, just as you have judged me forgiven. AMEN!

Respond: James says we are not to judge, lest we be judged. The flip side of that is to forgive as we have been forgiven. To repeat a challenge we've already done, tell someone that you forgive them out loud today. Do not hold their sin against them.

Receive: You may fear that Jesus' shed blood is not enough to pay for all your sins. But hear this Word from the Holy Spirit Himself: "For as many of you as were baptized into Christ have put on Christ" (Gal. 5:27). The Spirit says you are clothed in Christ. God no longer sees you as a guilty sinner but as one clothed in His beloved Son. With Him He is well pleased. Therefore, with you, He is well pleased for Christ's sake.

THE PATIENCE OF JOB

> *Brothers, as an example of patience in the face of suffering, take the prophets who spoke in the name of the Lord. As you know, we consider blessed those who have persevered. You have heard of Job's perseverance and have seen what the Lord finally brought about. The Lord is full of compassion and mercy.*

James 5:10–11

Job's story is not an unfamiliar one. It is the story of why. Why would God allow/cause suffering? Why won't God make the pain go away? Where is God in the midst of all this pain? Job's life was a good life. He had family and friends and a good job. God had granted him a seemingly unshakeable faith—that is, until Satan came along and tested God. He told God that if Job's blessings were removed, then Job would curse God and reject his faith. God allowed Satan to pretty much do everything to Job but kill him. Job, from the pit of despair, wanted answers: "Why would you allow this, oh Lord!?" Job, it seems, was putting God on trial!

Job may be the oldest book in the whole Bible, which means that this questioning of God is nothing new. Job may be one of the first to ask why of God, and he is certainly not the last. In fact, the very same cry is found on the lips of our dying Lord while hanging on the cross: "My God, my God, *why* have you forsaken me?" (Mark 15:34; cf. Ps. 22:1). Jesus, like Job and perhaps like you, received no immediate answer.

We desperately want to know why. Why do we suffer? Why is there evil in the world? Why would a good God not intervene? But have you considered that maybe we are not meant to know why? Ask yourself, "Even if I knew why, would it solve my problems?" Perhaps if God wanted us to know why, He would have told us. Perhaps He hasn't told us because He knows better.

Though we may not get the answer to the why of forsakenness, God does not remain silent. The response we receive is far better than we could ever hope or imagine!

Job attempts to put God on trial when suddenly, God shows up! God comes to Job and turns the tables on him: "Brace yourself like a man, I will question you, and you shall answer me!" (Job 38:3). God goes on to show Job that there are just some things beyond our comprehension. Job repents and the Lord has mercy on Job. "The Lord blessed the latter part of Job's life more than the first" (Job 42:12). Job went through hell and cried out to the Lord, and the Lord showed up and gave the gift of a new life.

This is a picture of what is accomplished for us through Christ on the cross. He is forsaken by God, taking all our sin and shame away, and three days later, He rose again to eternal life. With that resurrection, He promises that He will raise us with Him on the last day.

We will face suffering, pain, and death in this life. Why? Who knows? But God shows up in Christ Jesus for you! That means our suffering does not lead to eternal death or God forsakenness, for Christ is risen for you! So, though we may never get at the reasons for our pain, the one thing we do know for certain is that, in Christ, we are redeemed, and He is making all things right.

Repent: Heavenly Father, your thoughts are not my thoughts, and your ways are not my ways. Forgive me for not trusting your thoughts or your ways. Teach me to trust in you through my trials and struggles by keeping my eyes fixed on your Son Jesus who endured the cross for me and will raise me up with Him on the last day. Give me the perseverance of Job. AMEN.

Respond: Pray today for all those suffering from earthquakes, floods, hurricanes, tornadoes, and so on. Ask the Lord how you might help the people who suffer in such tragedies.

Receive: Though the Lord has not given you all the answers to your questions, He has given you the promise of the resurrection. What you are facing will be made right through the blood of the Lamb. So that, one day, when He returns, you will rise and sing and rejoice! Your life, like this world that is so wrecked in sin, will be made new. Already you have been declared righteous for Christ's sake, and one day, after your skin has been thus destroyed, you will rise and, in your flesh, you will see God!

YES AND NO

> *Above all, my brothers, do not swear—not by heaven or by earth or by anything else. Let your "Yes" be yes, and your "No," no, or you will be condemned.*

James 5:12

The Old Testament prophet Isaiah was once caught up into God's heavenly throne room. One glance at the glory of God drove him to despair because of his sinfulness. Isaiah said, "'Woe to me!' I cried. 'I am ruined! For I am a man of unclean lips, and I live among a people of unclean lips, and my eyes have seen the King, the LORD Almighty'" (Isa. 6:5). The sin that caused Isaiah the most fear was a dirty mouth! His lips, and the lips of his people, were unclean. Here is the almighty God who speaks creation into existence, who declares judgment on all sin, who kills and gives life with the Word of His mouth. He is seated in glory before lowly Isaiah, a man whose lips have known lies, blasphemies, cursing, and gossip. Seeing this heavenly vision causes Isaiah's unclean lips to cry out in despair!

The words we find on our lips are an expression of what is in our hearts. If our lips continually pour out praise for God, then the heart has received the gift of faith. St. Paul says, "For it is with your heart that you believe and are justified, and it is with your mouth that you confess and are saved" (Rom. 10:10). But if our lips continually pour out gossip, slander, and bitterness, then our hearts are shown to be sinful: "Not a word from their mouth can be trusted; their heart is filled with destruction" (Ps. 5:9). If our lips constantly boast of our righteousness, but our lives boast of sin, then our lips are unclean. But if our lips are found repenting, then our heart is shown to have faith in the Word.

We need to have our mouths washed out and our hearts renewed. As Isaiah sat in the presence of the Almighty, God sent an angel to touch Isaiah's lips with a burning coal from the altar. This coal was God's means of purifying Isaiah's lips and preparing his mouth to preach. The Lord has purified our hearts by washing us in baptism and placing His very body and blood in our mouths every Sunday. Our unclean hearts have been purified by the forgiving Word God has spoken through Christ. Our hearts have been cleansed, so our mouth may bring forth praise!

With purified hearts and lips, our speech to others reflects that of the One who has purified us. Our words are to be trustworthy, our promises fulfilled. Our "yes" should be yes and our "no" should be no. This is, after all, how God speaks His promises of forgiveness and mercy to us in Christ Jesus. "For no matter how many promises God has made, they are 'Yes' in Christ. And so through him the 'Amen' is spoken by us to the glory of God" (2 Cor. 1:20). Yes! You're forgiven and made pure through the blood of Christ! Amen!

Repent: Forgive me, gracious Father, for I am a person of unclean lips from a people of unclean lips. My words do not always reflect your glory and your grace. Teach me to train my tongue to sing your praises and speak the truth in love to my neighbors. AMEN.

Respond: Fulfill a yet-unfulfilled promise. Or if you have no unfulfilled promises that you can think of, make a promise and carry it out before next week.

Receive: This Sunday when you go to the Lord's Supper, God will not use a burning coal to purify your lips. He will instead purify you with the very body and blood of Jesus in the bread and wine. When you take, eat, and drink, when that blessed food hits your lips, hear the promise of the angel in your ears, "Behold, this has touched your lips; your guilt is taken away, and your sin atoned for" (Isa. 6:7).

THE LANGUAGE OF FAITH

> *Is any one of you in trouble? He should pray. Is anyone happy? Let him sing songs of praise. Is any one of you sick? He should call the elders of the church to pray over him and anoint him with oil in the name of the Lord. And the prayer offered in faith will make the sick person well; the Lord will raise him up. If he has sinned, he will be forgiven.*

James 5:13–15

Prayer is the language of faith. Prayer is the recognition that we are not self-reliant, autonomous beings, but in fact, we are dependent on God for all things. With good intentions, some have misquoted the Bible as saying that God will never give us anything we can't handle. Prayer is recognition that this is not the case. We can't handle this life on our own and so depend on God for everything: salvation, provision, oxygen, and so on. All good gifts come from the gracious hand of a loving Father. He handles everything. Prayer is not an aimless crying out to some greater power in the sky, but the humble, reverent approach of a sanctified sinner toward our Father, through the Son, in the power of the Holy Spirit. Prayer believes that Jesus was graciously correct and good in letting us call God our Father, and it acts on that belief.

We run into trouble when we begin to think that prayer is a command given to God instead of a gift given by Him. Prayer is not a demand we make on the Almighty. There are some false teachers who say that faith is a power we have, and prayer is the exercising of that power. So, they say, "If you have enough faith, God will give you whatever you want." That is the kind of faith the devil would have us desire. The prayer of faith doesn't test God, saying, "If you are really there, prove it by answering me." The prayer of faith is not self-seeking: "God, in Jesus' name I pray you give me a bigger house and a fancier car." We cannot think of prayer as the means by which we get God to do our bidding. So, Jesus teaches us to pray, "*Thy* will be done, on earth as it is in heaven" (emphasis mine; Matt. 6:10).

Faithful prayer is prayed with eyes fixed on the cross, knowing that the God we pray to has loved us so much that He sent His only Son to die for our sins and given us eternal life. There we see that God is for us, He is on our side. So, when we are in trouble, we can trust He will hear our prayers. When we are happy, we know He alone deserves our prayers of thanks. When we are sick, we know He will hear our prayers and the prayers of our brothers and sisters who cry out on our behalf. When we sin and cry out for mercy, we know we'll be forgiven for Jesus' sake. Faithful prayers are prayers formed, shaped, and given by a gracious God.

Repent: Merciful Father, forgive me for my misguided and self-serving prayers. Teach me to trust you more and to pray in faith. Like the disciples of your Son, I need to be taught to pray by Jesus. Thank you for graciously hearing my prayer, Father. AMEN.

Respond: For the next week, read a psalm every day and spend five minutes in prayer. Try to develop a regular habit of prayer beyond that week. If you need help, please contact your pastor or use your Small Catechism as a guide!

Receive: Jesus ever lives to intercede on your behalf. That means He sits before the Father in heaven, praying for you as your High Priest and as the sacrifice for your sins. You are not alone when you pray for forgiveness. Jesus prays the same. And the Father has listened and is pleased with Christ's sacrifice for your sake. Jesus prays, "Father, forgive them!" And the Father responds, "For your sake, they are forgiven."

PRAYER AND HEALING

> *And the prayer offered in faith will make the sick person well; the Lord will raise him up. If he has sinned, he will be forgiven. Therefore confess your sins to each other and pray for each other so that you may be healed. The prayer of a righteous man is powerful and effective. Elijah was a man just like us. He prayed earnestly that it would not rain, and it did not rain on the land for three and a half years. Again he prayed, and the heavens gave rain, and the earth produced its crops.*

James 5:15–18

These are wonderful verses! And yet, how difficult they are to believe. Are God's promises to answer prayer as good as James makes them sound? Will our cries of faith really move God to heal us and forgive us? Yes! As we said yesterday, it is not because our faith is so strong or because our prayers are so inspiring. It is because He is so gracious that God will answer our prayers!

We must be careful when we read these passages, however. Too often they are read with a "fast-food order" mentality. We live in a fast-food culture where we want our food to be given to us within minutes of making the order. We bring this mentality to our prayers. "Lord, I am sick. Please heal me . . . NOW!" Or "Lord, my loved one is dying. Please restore their life . . . NOW!" When we pray like this, we've made our order to God for the healing; now we simply need to pull forward to the second window and have Him give it to us in a timely fashion.

But then our prayers seemingly go unanswered. Prolonged sickness, suffering, and death do their best to convince us that God is, at best, not listening or, at worst, not keeping His promises. James' words to us today seem almost cold and insulting. We worry that perhaps our faith isn't strong enough and that is why God has not answered us immediately.

Our culture of immediate gratification struggles with the patience required by prayer. God's timing seems slow to us, and prayer can often be a hard lesson in patience. It makes sense that one of the most popular prayers we find in the Bible is "How long, O Lord?" But as we saw a few days ago with Job, God's answer to the "How long?" question is full of great hope. For though we will endure much pain and hardship in this life, Christ will return to grant the very healing we have prayed for. Sins will be abolished, bodily ailments will be healed, and dead loved ones who died in the faith will be raised to everlasting life with Christ. Our short time of suffering will lead to an eternity of joy in Christ. Our prayers will be answered.

Jesus Himself knew such suffering as He sweat blood in the garden. God called Christ to endure the cross, and often He will have us face hardships that drive us to prayer. But the worst such hardships can do is drive us to death in Christ, which is actually victory! Death was conquered by Christ when He rose on Easter morning. The answer to your prayers is found on Easter morning at the empty tomb, where Christ has promised to meet you when He returns. The promise is true: "Weeping may remain for the night, but rejoicing comes in the morning" (Ps. 30:5). So, with the church we cry, "Come Lord Jesus! AMEN!"

Repent: Father of all mercies, I praise you that you hear my prayers and answer them in love. Forgive me for my impatience and lack of trust in your will. Help me look to Jesus' empty tomb with great anticipation knowing that, when He returns and raises me up, all my prayers will be answered. AMEN!

Respond: In your prayer time, learn to pray the Lord's Prayer. Use each petition as a guiding outline for your whole prayer. (If you need to know what the different petitions are, see Luther's Small Catechism.)

Receive: Every time you pray the Lord's Prayer, you pray for your forgiveness. Hear this good news: Right now, because Jesus Christ died for you, God has answered that prayer for you. You are forgiven!

SAVED FROM DEATH

> *My brothers, if one of you should wander from the truth and someone should bring him back, remember this: Whoever turns a sinner from the error of his way will save him from death and cover over a multitude of sins.*

James 5:19–20

With these words, James concludes what is likely the earliest New Testament writing. And what a note to end on! The very Gospel itself! Through our journey, James has called to our attention many voices that try to drown out God's Word so we would wander away from His truth. False teachers arise trying to tell us that Christ is not sufficient for our salvation, and they offer different plans. The riches of this world try to tell us that there is a better way of living than suffering with Christ. Our own pride and self-righteousness tell us we don't need to listen to God's Word and that other people are merely a means to an end. All these voices James has silenced along the way so that we end up at the foot of the cross, once again, ready to hear this good news: Jesus died to save you from death, and His blood covers all your sins.

This is the message that brings salvation. The preaching of Christ crucified for sinners is the very Word of God that creates and sustains faith in our
hearts. We need this message constantly placed in our ears by someone else,
lest we grow distracted by false teachers, worldly temptations, and our own
pride. By placing this Word in our ears, the Holy Spirit secures Christ in our
hearts. This gives us great hope and confidence before God and the world.

In this world, however, there are many who are distracted. They are listening to the other voices. Some have walked away from the faith. Some have
never known the truth in the first place. If hearing the message of Jesus brings
the light of God's love, then the messages that our friends in the world are
hearing darkens them to the truth. "Faith," St. Paul says, "comes from hearing the message" (Rom. 10:17). But many don't hear the message of forgiveness and so remain in the darkness. "How, then, can they call on the one they
have not believed in? And how can they believe in the one of whom they have
not heard? And how can they hear without someone preaching to them?"
(Rom. 10:14).

People in this world will not believe the Gospel unless someone tells them
the Gospel. They don't know that God has forgiven their sins in Christ Jesus.
They don't know that they have been reconciled to God through Christ's
blood. They don't know that Jesus rose again for their salvation. How can
they unless someone tells them?

You know the truth. The truth has set you free. You belong to Jesus. You
are baptized. Your sins are forgiven. You have been given new life in Christ.
God has promised you a place with Christ for eternity. All these promises
Christ has secured for you in His death and resurrection. He's done it for
everyone else too. So tell them, for *heaven's* sake! That message from the lips
of your mouth is full of the Jesus who will save them, just as He has saved you!

Repent: Father, forgive me for not speaking your Gospel boldly. I have kept this public news to myself as if it was a private belief. Give me a mouth to declare your forgiveness and love to the whole world with boldness, confidence, and joy. AMEN.

Respond: Invite a friend to church. Tell them you go because you know that there, of all places, you will receive what the world will not give, forgiveness for free.

Receive: This is the good news: God has sent His Son to die on the cross to pay for all your sins. He rose again on the third day for your sake. God has declared you righteous. You are forgiven for Christ's sake! Death is defeated, you are free! AMEN!

BIBLIOGRAPHY

Luther, Martin. *Luther's Works*. Vol. 35, *Word and Sacrament I*, edited by Jaroslav Jan Pelikan, Hilton C. Oswald, and Helmut T. Lehmann. Philadelphia: Fortress, 1999.

———. "Prefaces to the New Testament." In *Martin Luther's Basic Theological Writings*, edited by Timothy Lull. Minneapolis: Fortress, 1989.

———. "Prefaces to the Old Testament." In *Martin Luther's Basic Theological Writings*, edited by Timothy Lull. Minneapolis: Fortress, 1989.

Scaer, David P. *James the Apostle of Faith: A Primary Christological Epistle for the Persecuted Church*. St. Louis: Concordia, 1983.

CPSIA information can be obtained
at www.ICGtesting.com
Printed in the USA
LVHW110232040220
645692LV00003B/68